Generation Now
Millennials Call for Social Change

To the Next Wave of Changemakers

Copyright @ 2018 by Christine Henseler
All rights reserved.

For information about permission to reproduce selections from this book, write to GenerationNow@union.edu

This project was developed by
Christine Henseler
at Union College
Schenectady, NY 12308

Book cover by Hana Brown, illustrated on her phone
Printed in the United States of America, through CreateSpace.

ISBN-13: 978-1720610229
ISBN-10: 1720610223

Generation Now
Millennials Call for Social Change

Emily Adams
Tayor Allen
Randi Broadwell
Hana Brown
Megan Brown
Kaitlyn Connor
Sasha Currie
Giuseppe De Spuches
Jacques Pierre Treguier
Hamza Ghumman
Phoebe Hallahan
Brooke Mackenzie
Anna Mahony
Kate Osterholtz
Ademilola Oyetuga
Hayden Paneth
Kathleen Sinatra

Guided by Christine Henseler
UNION COLLEGE ~ 2018

ABOUT THIS BOOK

*"The world changes according to the way people see it,
and if you alter, even by a millimeter, the way ...
people look at reality, then you can change it."*
~ James Baldwin

In the spring of 2018, a group of Union College students took a class called "Millennials and Social Change" taught by Prof. Christine Henseler. They were in for a surprise.

They registered for a course about the rise of the everyday changemaker. It was a class that focused on the current student generation, the Millennials (b. 1980-2000), and the changes they wished to see in their lives and in their communities.

Ten weeks later, the students in this class had risen do become changemakers themselves. With honesty, passion, and dedication, they had written personal stories meant to inspire and give hope to others. Their collective calls for change have become this book.

These are their fearless stories.

PAYING IT FORWARD

100% of this book's proceeds are donated to C.O.C.O.A. House

Located in Schenectady, NY, the "Children of Our Community Open to Achievement" program was founded by a Union College alumna as a way to give back to the community through tutoring and positive role modeling aimed at improving the academic, social, and life skills of local youth. The program also provides college students with leadership development and active learning based on community engagement and service.

C.O.C.O.A. House is a place that fosters young people to become imaginative and critical thinkers, lifelong learners, and responsible and involved citizens in a diverse, global community. As such, C.O.C.O.A. House places a high value on respect, self-reliance, empowerment, and perseverance.

THANKS
Without You There Would Be No Us

We found out pretty quickly that to self-publish a book in 10 weeks, it takes a lot more than 19 brains and a spectacular idea. Without the knowledge and resources from those who helped us along the way, this project would not have been possible.

We'd like to thank:

Jeff Goronkin and Caroline Boardman at Urban Co-Works, for the privilege of working in their office space every week.

Margaret Graham, Director of the Union College Scholars Program, for the funds that kept our stomachs happy.

Blair Raymond, Senior Director of External Relations at Union College, for funding our shuttle transportation.

The Union College Transportation Department for picking us up and dropping us off.

Katie Cusack at *The Alt, The Capital Region's Alternative Newsweekly,* for imparting her writing wisdom.

Jennifer Fredricks, Dean of Academic Departments and Programs at Union College, for funds to publish this book.

Special thanks to Union College for the creative freedom to run this non-traditional class on "Millennials and Social Change."

CONTENTS

Introduction: *You Get Out What You Put in*	1
Emily Adams: *My Trauma Shapes Me, But I'm Not Defined By It*	6
Taylor Allen: *"Labor for Learning": Understanding Immigration Through Family Stories*	12
Randi Broadwell: *Wanting the Cake and Eating it Too*	22
Hana Brown: *Conversations With A Goat Girl*	31
Megan Brown: *Who Said It Was "Daddy's Money?"*	38
Kaitlyn Connor: *No Child Left Behind…Except You, You, and You*	46
Sasha Currie: *OMG, Please Kill Me Now*	54
Giuseppe De Spuches: *We Don't Need No Education*	61
Jacques Pierre Treguier: *A Solution to Pollution*	71
Hamza Ghumman: *When They Don't Take You Seriously*	79
Phoebe Hallahan: *My Television Romance*	87
Brooke Mackenzie: *Can You Hear Me or Am I Crazy?: Breaking The Stigma on Mental Health*	97
Anna Mahony: *Life in Plastic is Not Fantastic*	104
Kate Osterholtz: *The Birds and Bees and Everything in Between*	115
Ademilola Oyetuga: *The Ones Left Behind: How America is Failing the Poor*	123
Hayden Paneth: *The Crossed Out, Torn Out Pages*	136
Kathleen Sinatra: *"But You Look Fine!": Navigating High School with an Invisible, Chronic Illness*	144
Epilogue: *Continue the Wave of Change*	156
The Authors	159
A Special Thanks: *To Christine*	160
Notes and Bibliography	166
Photos & More	184

A LITTLE TASTE

Preface: *You Get Out What You Put in*

Emily Adams: *My Trauma Shapes Me, But I'm Not Defined By It*

By sharing a personal narrative, Emily explores her experience with relationship violence and puts her story into a #MeToo context, a movement that has contributed greatly to the definition of the Millennial generation. Weaving together her past, present, and future with statistics from various studies on harassment, assault, and abuse in both public and private spaces, Emily aims to give hope to other survivors and to better educate the next generation on these topics.

Taylor Allen: *"Labor for Learning": Understanding Immigration through Family Stories*

Immigrants are often painted as alien and misplaced in a land meant for foreigners. This can lead to questions of identity and belonging. Through interviews with several first-generation Americans and her own mother, Taylor explores the complex nature of international identities and the forces that make them so hard to understand. Through these deeply personal accounts, she encourages a shift in perspective to normalize the immigrant experience and humanize those which are perceived to be outsiders by supporting fair legislation and advocacy organizations.

Randi Broadwell: *Wanting the Cake and Eating it Too*

Randi sheds some light on the unconventional woman. Being called an unconventional woman and unladylike throughout Randi's life inspired her to approach some of the stigmas surrounding the issues of these 'masculinized women' of the Millennial generation. What values should be seen in a woman? How has it affected them in the home, workforce, and how, in Randi's opinion, should we all begin to combat this issue.

Hana Brown: *Conversations With A Goat Girl*

It is easy to not involve a child in real world issues, dismissing them as too young. It's presented as 'preserving their innocence,' but in reality, they are being shut out of "real" conversations. Working with children led Hana to understand the importance of honest conversations. A goat-loving girl would be the key to shifting her mindset on how children view the world, and how an open conversation may be the best tool for a child to prepare themselves for the future.

Megan Brown: *Who Said It Was "Daddy's Money?"*

Living in the year 2018, one would think that perceptions of men and women in society are beginning to equalize, but we're not as far along as some people believe. Megan shares her story of growing up in a gender non-traditional household and the experiences she has encountered as a young woman in society. She completes her message with her own research. Megan hopes to encourage women not to be limited by societal perceptions, to be confident in their dreams and aspirations, and to inspire the elimination of any possibility of having an asterisk next to their successes: that they were good "for a girl."

Kaitlyn Connor: *No Child Left Behind...Except You, You, and You*

We live in a very hypocritical society. We are constantly fighting for equality, yet when it comes down to it, numerous groups are consistently overlooked. In New York State, the "No Child Left Behind" clause helped guarantee that children with learning disabilities wouldn't fall behind other classmates. However, there are still children being "left behind." Kaitlyn shares her experiences with the United Cerebral Palsy School, expressing what she has learned about education for children with severe disabilities and what needs to be done, while additionally sharing her own call to action.

Sasha Currie: *OMG, Please Kill Me Now*

Throughout social media and various streaming sites, suicide is often romanticized for the purpose of pure entertainment. Most perpetuate the idea that there is a concrete reason behind someone committing suicide. Sasha hopes to eradicate these notions as well as the stigma associated with individuals who seek help through therapy or counseling. She also hopes to encourage other ways in which individuals in society could work towards opening discussions of suicide prevention. This could then aid in decreasing rates of suicide in the U.S.

Giuseppe De Spuches: *We Don't Need No Education*

Education is often taken for granted by wealthier communities around the world. However, learning is much more valuable than we might realize. Not receiving an education or understanding how the world works around us, which is common in many underdeveloped countries, will slow down our development as human beings. So what can we do? What has been done? Giuseppe asks: is there a solution to this problem? And if there is, can we expect to see it fulfilled in our lifetime?

Jacques Pierre Treguier: *A Solution to Pollution*

The world is full of opportunity for good. Pollution is one of the greatest threats to the well-being of humanity. In JP's opinion, encouraging entrepreneurship and innovation in education systems can accelerate the process of developing solutions to help us better control our mistreatment of the environment.

Hamza Ghumman: *When They Don't Take You Seriously*

Developing countries lack a complete education. Hamza focuses on Pakistan, where he went to school from the 6th to 10th grade. School there never felt like a place where he was growing as an individual. The frustration he felt was shared by countless other students, but he was fortunate enough to have the resources to come back to the United States. Hamza wants to see schools become a place where students are learning outside the classroom, through extra curricular activities and clubs that students will take initiative forming. This he believes to be a first step to reforming the educational system of Pakistan.

Phoebe Hallahan: *My Television Romance*

As Millennials and Gen Z'ers, we are known as the virtual generations: always attached to our devices, which is usually perceived as a negative. However, television has had a strong positive impact on Phoebe. She would almost go so far as to say it changed her life, and no doubt has had strong impacts on others and can continue to do so.

Brooke Mackenzie: *Can You Hear Me or Am I Crazy?: Breaking The Stigma on Mental Health*

With a society supposedly as evolved as ours, why is it that people are still being quieted for daring to share their emotions? At what point will it be acceptable for a person to have feelings and be given a platform to positively express them. While it may seem trivial, this emotional oppression has led to a wide-spread issue of stigmatizing mental and emotional health. As a result we see children routinely committing self-harm and people being prescribed medical cocktails. While the issue is complex in nature, the solution is relatively simple: talk about it. Brooke's challenge to people is to own their whole self and see the beauty in everyone's courage to fight the idea of there being a "normal."

Anna Mahony: *Life in Plastic is Not Fantastic*

Humans are polluting the world. Climate change is becoming an ever-pressing issue that is not garnering as much attention and change as it should. Anna shares her story of learning the importance of sustainability and becoming passionate about the environment through experiences growing up and studying in New Zealand. Specifically, she discusses why education about climate change is important and the small ways people can make a difference in the world.

Kate Osterholtz: *The Birds and Bees and Everything In Between*

Kate's story explores how to be comfortable with the uncomfortable. Through a personal narrative, she discusses the taboo topic of Sex-Ed and normalizing the conversation around all aspects of sex. Through an anecdotal story, as well as evidence from Dutch researchers, she explores what it truly means to be on the cusp of one's own sexuality. By making this more of an everyday conversation and enforcing comprehensive sex education at a young age, Kate hopes to influence Millennials to make informed choices which develop healthy relationships for generations to come.

Ademilola Oyetuga: *The Ones Left Behind: How America is Failing the Poor*

In this year of 2018, why are low income/poverty levels still an issue? Why does the quality of education that children receive vary so much, allowing some children to succeed and others to fall behind? What can we do about these problems, asks Ademilola. By providing quality education to kids in underfunded areas, we can work to end the larger issue of poverty in the United States. Education needs to be seen as a basic right for children: independent of socioeconomic status, race, and neighborhood. The children are the future, so let's work to help them live in a more equitable one.

Hayden Paneth: *The Crossed Out, Torn Out Pages*

Born and raised in Brooklyn, NY, Hayden shares her personal narrative of a struggle between isolation and education. Despite residing in NYC, this Hasidic girl was isolated from American culture. This article provides an insider's peek at what it was like growing up confined to the rules, separated from mainstream education, and how Hayden advocates for change in government policy to oversee the quality of Hasidic educational institutions.

Kathleen Sinatra: *"But you look fine!": Navigating High School with an Invisible, Chronic Illness*

Humans crave tangibility. But, when your illness is chronic and invisible, navigating life as a high school student can be challenging. Through personal narrative, Kathleen describes her experience as a high school student dealing with chronic Lyme disease. In doing so, she details changes that must be made in the high school education system so as to better support students with invisible illnesses and prepare and empower educators to do the same.

Epilogue: *Continue the Wave of Change*

DIY

Throughout this book, we include spaces such as these.
They are meant for you to arrive at your own answers.

1   Generation Now: Millennials Call for Social Change

INTRODUCTION

You Get Out What You Put In

    Millennials: a generation that was born and raised in an era of information and global communications, where even the smallest injustice, in the smallest town, in the smallest country, triggers a call for respect. In our day, everything is relevant and everyone deserves attention. Everyone is expected to know everything. Anything is possible, ironically making new discoveries seem impossible. So how can we care about everything when we have an almost overwhelming amount of information at our fingertips? How can we make an impact in this world if every time we tackle one issue, another one seems to arise?

    We are a group of students from Union College in Schenectady, NY. To some, the fact that we are young may invalidate this book. How can we inspire social change at such a young age? What do we even know about social change?

    It is our personal experiences that give voice to our generation. Our stories act as a thread that connects each generation together - a force that is more powerful than age. So, while we may eat gummy bears and laugh as we work, the narratives we share explore issues that are of relevance to everyone in our world. We are Millennials; we are the current generation of social change.

Millennials are the largest generation thus far and, arguably, the most diverse, open-minded, and apt to break the status quo. The infinite range of information that we have access to is not necessarily bad. It opens our world to infinite possibilities for change, infinite calls for action, infinite ways that humankind can provide support to others and the planet. It is innate human emotions that we hope to evoke in you, the reader, that connect us all, regardless of age or experience. They connect us to each other, to our fellow Millennials, and to other generations. We feel it is our duty as the next generation of changemakers to ensure that our change is positive and promotes a better world for the generations to come.

The Millennial generation is intrigued by the concept of social change. Yet, defining this commonly-used term is difficult, but essential. In the context of this book, "social change" has nothing but positive connotations. When attempting to define it ourselves, we had varying definitions. One wrote, "social change can be made both in intangible ways, such as by changing attitudes and behaviors, as well as in more tangible ways, like changing laws and policies". Another stated that, "social change is about identifying a problem and working towards a solution that improves the lifestyle of those who were originally affected by it". Change is constant. Every contributor to this book is passionate about helping the world in one way or another. We all crave the potentiality of shaping change regarding social issues covered in this book.

What makes this book different from all other books on social change that seem to spew idyllic sounding narratives? Well, for starters, we literally signed up for a course entitled "Millennials and Social Change." Every Wednesday, for ten weeks, we took a shuttle to a professional office space in downtown Schenectady, where we workshopped and collaborated. We were determined to make the best possible product. Guided by our professor, Dr. Christine Henseler, we learned about social change and were inspired by fellow Millennial changemakers.

The class was very much student-driven, embodying the seemingly cliché, yet abundantly accurate quote, "you get out what you put in." We learned about the need for increasing educational opportunities through a book by Adam Braun called *The Promise of a Pencil: How an Ordinary Person Can Create Extraordinary Change*. We were taught the importance of combating excessive waste through the film *The Clean Bin Project*, directed by Grant Baldwin. We were inspired by the journey documented in *Living on One Dollar*, directed by Chris Temple, Zach Ingrasci, and Sean Leonard. With this knowledge in hand, we were prepared to start our own process of changemaking. The creation of this book has the ability to inspire change through a combination of academia and humanity that has never been seen before.

Throughout this journey, each one of us Millennial changemakers went through our own process. We quickly realized the gargantuan task we were taking on. It would not be easy and we each grappled with this challenge in our own way. For some, choosing which movement they were passionate about seemed impossible. For others, it was coping with trauma or hardship and having the courage to share that story. We were reminded that our voices matter and that our generation has the capacity to ignite that change that we all desperately wish to see.

This book did not come together flawlessly. We faced obstacles, large and small, every day. It was those obstacles that helped us learn, and without which we would have produced a very different book. Combining 18 brains is easier said than done. It was inevitable that when communicating our different ideas, we were bound to bump heads, but it was those bumps that shaped the book and made it that much more authentic.

At the college age, each student is bursting with ideas that, if unsatisfied, will likely explode. Despite this, all of our desires were met through compromise. Compromise is imperative in effectively completing a task, and likewise, in making change. Whether that be socially, governmentally, economically, or culturally, being able to listen, speak up, and have the willingness to set aside your ideas for a better one is what creates a successful changemaker.

The goal of this book is to educate and inspire, no matter the age demographic that it reaches. With our stories, we hope to connect personally with everyone who reads it. We worked tirelessly to shed light on issues that would inspire older generations, hopefully learning something from those younger, and conversely, to encourage young people to feel empowered, knowing that they can influence positive change.

Social change will not end with the creation of this book. Instead, it will continue in a cyclical fashion, giving inspiration and voice to other Millennials and the next wave of changemakers. Everyone can make social change. The creation of this book is proof.

In order for this change to last, however, it must to be maintained. Together we can accomplish this task - one person, one community at a time.

DIY

Write down two or three topics that you are passionate about. Why do they matter to you?

EMILY ADAMS

"Stranger, if you passing meet me and desire to speak to me, why should you not speak to me? And why should I not speak to you?"
~ Walt Whitman

What is a characteristic that you would like to change in yourself?

If I could live more in the present than the future, I could truly experience life in the moment instead of constantly anticipating what will come, thus recognizing the small gifts in my daily life.

What world do I want to live in?

My ideal world is diverse, educated, liberated, and harmonious. I firmly believe all four qualities can be achieved and maintained in a single society.

Why is social change such an important issue, especially today having so much information available all the time?

With the constant availability of information and the instant gratification associated with accessing such information, I believe our generation must remember the obstacle of physically reaching out and connecting with others to create change. Technology limits our ability to make tangible change in our world. Online storytelling allows for our voices to be heard, but real change must be made through human connection.

My Trauma Shapes Me, But I'm Not Defined By It

Emily Adams

I have always been a hopeless romantic, spending hours with my dolls in my youth, dressing them carefully and arranging their perfect marriages in various make-believe situations. This love for love continued into my real life when I entered high school and was ready to fumble my way to adulthood. But, my spritely dreams of having a cute high school boyfriend came crashing down my freshman year when I became a statistic.

Without realizing it, I had lost myself not *in* someone but *by* someone because of relationship violence. Love was fleeting and I receded into a shameful, dark place after I was able to process what I had endured in the relationship. The abuse ruined me. My boyfriend had repeatedly violated me physically, emotionally, and mentally. I was publicly humiliated as well; he spread nude images of me to the entire school, and I have no idea where they might be in cyberspace now. I was blackmailed by my boyfriend to keep quiet, yet was backstabbed anyway. Everyone knew what I had done, not what he had done to me.

I was blamed by my classmates, friends, and family; *no one* blamed my abusive boyfriend for the trauma. I was a fourteen-year-old child, yet even my family disowned me. As my mental health declined at the hands of the world's rejection, I felt sucked into a spiral and isolated myself, reaching out to no one for help.

The years of self-loathing tired me, and somehow, I snapped a few years later. I grew sick of being a victim and began faking happiness until I felt it again. I dressed in the brightest richly-patterned clothes I could find, splurging on designer brands and studying the hardest I could. Instead of focusing on my history, I would give my school something to talk about. I would prove everyone in my school, community, and home wrong. I was successful. I was *not* a slut or whore. I did not let my mistakes define me. I was artistically and academically talented; I had become more than a statistic.

Soon after I made the decision to be happy, the rest of the world aligned. She too had withstood enough. TIME Person of the Year 2017 were the Silence Breakers: the women who stood up and voiced accusations against powerful men who had harassed and abused them.[1] October 15, 2017 was the beginning of #MeToo, the hashtag that fueled Twitter, the media, the government, and the scientific community to pay attention.[2] Studies were conducted, finding that 81% of women and 43% of men have experienced sexual harassment or assault.[3] By age 17, 57% of these women had their first incidence.[4] I had not been alone when I was abused, and I am not alone as I continue to heal.

To the amazement of older generations, Millennials are changing the statistics. In 2011, the rate of serious partner violence against women decreased 72% from 1994 to 1.6 incidences per 1,000 women aged 12 and above.[5] Our society now listens to the voices of victims, but the comprehension and recognition of sexual assault is not complete. Underhanded compliments, demeaning behavior, catcalling, groping, manipulation, blackmail, and physical violence are all too frequently experienced in public and private spaces. Feelings of anxiety, abandonment, and insecurity are familiar to those who have experienced relationship violence (especially during formative adolescent years), but may come in unexplained periods during the relationship as well as later in life.[6]

Any woman who has experienced harassment, assault, or abuse knows the complex emotions associated with recovery much better than a scientific journal could ever describe.

Walking down the sidewalk is frightening for those who have been catcalled or stalked; forming relationships are difficult for those who have experienced relationship violence. I was uncomfortable with my own being, speaking in class, and approaching others after my experience. Forming a meaningful relationship was not possible because of my mental health and trauma. By the grace of God, through (slowly, but forcefully) healing myself, I clung to my romantic dreams and learned to trust and love another person fully. I have been blessed with someone who understands my trauma and sees me as more than my experience and more than a statistic.

As a survivor, recognizing the signs of relationship violence, sexual harassment, and sexual assault are most important to me as a means to help other women experiencing trauma. Perhaps if the #MeToo movement had happened my first year of high school, my future could have been different. Maybe, there would've been more support for me instead of victim-blaming. Because young adolescents do not typically experience workplace harassment and lack direct education on harassment, abuse, and violence, we as Millennials lack the skills to recognize them, resulting in the blaming of victims instead of perpetrators.[7]

We remain tolerant (something we *were* taught) and passive: just as I had, not grasping the presence of my abuse during the relationship and the extent of the trauma until after it had concluded. Through education by schools, parents, and the media alike, the societal perception and comprehension of these circumstances can be more easily identified, preventing the consequential manifestations of depression, anxiety, self-loathing, and distrust by survivors.

Millennial parents (34% of mothers, 35% of fathers) value teaching their children respect over any other trait or value.[8] The internal paradox I experience as a trauma survivor and hopeless romantic supports this finding, as self-respect is something I intend to teach my children. Parenthood is something I very much look forward to in life. My experiences, in combination with all the stories we hear about on the news in Hollywood or in our office or in the lives of our friends, have prepared me to facilitate conversations with my future children about personal respect and healthy (romantic and other) relationships.

Confidence and respect builds strong character, thus creating a better person. Although twisted to contemplate, I might not be the courageous, self-assured woman that I am today without enduring this trauma during my formative teenage years. The respect I permitted my battered self to have facilitated my personal growth. By allowing me to respect myself, I was able to heal and transform into a stronger woman who is not defined by her trauma. I anticipate my continued growth in the future, and I remain optimistic that my generation has the ability to do the same.

TAYLOR ALLEN

"The arc of the moral universe is long, but it bends toward justice."
~ Rev. Martin Luther King, Jr

Who am I?

I am a biology major with a focus on healthcare, public health, and Africana studies. My hobbies include microblogging, traveling, finding new music, and trying new restaurants.

How do I see myself as a changemaker?

I see myself as a changemaker with untapped potential. I see my ability to be influential especially in healthcare policy and health equity research. I hope to be able to make change through my career in public health, but also through my attention to my communities.

What world do I want to live in?

I want to live in a world where we are all respectful of each other's humanity, a place in which the ways in which we are different make us more alike than anything else, a world where all are seen as valuable based not only on their contributions to the economy. I want to live in a world where we respect diversity and enjoy diversity.

If you had to pick one musical artist to listen to for the rest of your life who would it be?

I could absolutely listen to Erykah Badu for the rest of my life. Her positive vibes and the characteristics of her music and personality are so relaxing and musically beautiful.

"Labor for Learning": Understanding Immigration through Family Stories

Taylor Allen

"Labor for learning before you grow old for learning is better than silver or gold. Silver and gold will soon pass away but a good education will never decay."

This saying has been passed down through my family for generations as a commitment to lifelong learning. It is the cause for the series of events that brought me to existence. Generally, we attribute the saying to my great-grandmother, known affectionately as Tita.

She was a woman who won dance competitions and made the best curry goat in the neighborhood. She was not a tall woman, though she was outspoken and independent. In the Jamaican dialect, we would say, "she likkle but she tallawah."

My mother was the last of her four siblings to immigrate to the United States at the age of 19. In 1980, all Pamela Elizabeth Hylton had to do to get her visa was meet once or twice with someone at the U.S. embassy to Jamaica. She immigrated soon after her high school graduation in September of that year.

Historically, the United States has maintained caps for immigrants from various countries throughout that world, even banning immigration from certain nations (see Chinese Exclusion Act, the McCarran-Walter Act and the Muslim Ban).[9] As a result, for generations, immigrants were from largely European nations and the growth of populations of immigrants of color remained small.[10]

When my mom was still a toddler in 1965, the U.S. was 15% non-white.[11] During the Civil Rights Movement, when people who already lived here were vying for equal treatment, there was a successful argument for more inclusive immigration policy.

By 2009, people of color in the United States had increased to 33% including immigrants and their descendants, like my family.[12] Being able to trace one's close ancestors to nations around the world is increasingly popular and welcome in many places. Yet, the idea of the "American" identity has been warped. Rather than embracing our national heritage as a nation of immigrants, many lament the progress that immigrants of color have made in diversifying our country.

Restructuring of immigration policy in the 1960s encouraged immigrants from around the world, including Asia, Africa and Eastern Europe. Most notably, the bill signed into law by President Johnson allowed for a system of sponsorship wherein individuals were able to advocate for the legal immigration of their immediate family members. This specific provision was vital in the immigration process of my family. Without it, immigration policies can provide a barrier to family unification.

To better understand my family's story, I spoke to a few students with a family history or personal history of immigration about their experiences as people with international-identities and hyphenated-Americans. First was Benni who considers Queens, NY her home. Benni's parents are ethnically Chinese and immigrated from Burma in 1990. Meghan-Hannah considers Fairfield, CT her home and is proud of her Indian-American heritage. Her parents immigrated separately to the United States in the 1990s after their marriage. Binta, a student born and raised in Guinea, joined her parents in the United States in 2013 to complete high school.

Today, the immigration process is much more difficult. Binta describes how her family has been separated and united from Guinea to the United States over a period of 14 years. My mom frequently thinks of how blessed she was to be able to immigrate in the 1980s before competition for immigration to the United States from Jamaica became more intense.

My mom describes her immigration experience as generally positive, though not a decision of her own: "It was for family reasons, I was brought here. Being the last child, we were brought here for a better life. My parents wanted us to have better access to education." In my social studies classes growing up, we were taught that immigration is a result of overlapping push and pull factors. Push factors are those that encourage immigrants to leave their nations of origin. Pull factors are those that attract immigrants to a particular nation.

Though it sounds cliché, most immigrants come to the United States for increased opportunities for themselves and their families.[13] Benni decided that her family's main pull factor for immigration was "upward social mobility" and her father's potential to "gain prestige."

To improve their socio-economic status, many immigrants sacrifice some part of their life or self in order to be successful in their new environment. Immigrant parents, like my own, often talk about the opportunities or circumstances they gave up in order to live here and assimilate into American society. For some, this may be visible markers of faith, like a religious head covering or talisman. For others, this can be the straining of family ties. Unfortunately, a few months after my mother's last trip to Jamaica, Tita passed away and there was no chance to say goodbye.

In addition to losing a sense of identity, a simple lack of cultural awareness in the United States impacted her experience. In 1980s New York City, West Indian identities (as my mom refers to them) were not well known. In applying for college, admissions counselors asked if her first language was English and she found that people did not respect her international identity.

Contrary to popular belief, the highest proportion of foreign-born individuals in the United States was reached in 1890 with 14.8 percent of residents born outside of the country compared to under 14 percent today.[14] Immigration rates have remained fairly stagnant recently, yet the current administration takes frequent opportunities to discredit the worthiness of immigrants from nations outside of Europe, especially those from Africa and the Americas.

Besides the underlying global economic factors that influence immigration, the United States (and other similar developed nations) is at fault for its own high rates of immigration due to the types of economic and foreign policies it has maintained.

Those that dismiss the real experiences of immigrants and their families often are unaware of the universal understandings that bring immigrants to the United States. For my mother, that was the promise of a quality education and a generalized "better life." For others, that may be financial prosperity or an escape from conditions in their nation of origin.

―――

I'm told that I resemble my great-grandmother Tita with my chocolate skin and smaller stature. Though my grandmother sees my "Jamaican-ness" and validates my hyphenated identity, embracing my "American-ness" was a challenge. In my experience, I am quick to identify my Jamaican heritage but refuse to identify as an unhyphenated-American.

Megan-Hannah felt differently. She strongly iden-tifies with her American identity as the nation where she was born. At college, she identifies more often as Indian because she "come[s] off as very Indian in America." Though underrepresented in media, people of color and immigrants are quickly reaching a majority position in the United States. It is telling that we are often stereotyped as being outsiders or immigrants regardless of immigration status in a nation we should consistently be able to call their own.

Combining an increasingly diverse immigration population with the lingering racism and classism that persists in the American public has helped shape the perceptions of generations of immigrants and their families. As a child of immigrants, especially Black immigrants, I am constantly reminded of how I cannot fit cleanly into the boxes which are supposed to define me. As a Jamaican-American born here, I will forever be American in Jamaica and Black in the United States, unless I decide to immigrate somewhere myself.

However, being a child of Black immigrants means being regularly ascribed as African American. This makes it impossible to separate my Caribbean-American experience from the African-American experience. In that sense, my ethnic background does not change my perceived race in the United States.

For me, being here requires a balance of retaining my ethnic background and contextualizing myself into the Black American experience.

Being both Black and of international parentage has shaped my perception of the "American identity."

———

A toxic American nationalism has led to anti-immigrant sentiment among certain groups. This perpetuates the racialized concept that allows certain groups to be considered American and continues to relegate others to the margins. For instance, Benni identifies herself as somewhere in between her American identity and her Chinese-Burmese identity. Being an immigrant, especially a child of a non-White immigrant, can lead many to have a sense of vague international identity paired with a complex relationship with their "American-ness."

My mother sees this differently, she is happy to be able to identify with two places at once and to be able to embrace her "dual-identity." Identity is a deeply personal and fluid understanding of oneself. Though it is intrinsically tied to environment and societal norms, we all are able to decide, to a certain extent, who we are.

In a nation where immigrants are supposed to be celebrated and supported in their quest for the American dream, and where diverse ethnic and racial backgrounds will be the majority with a few decades, we have to grapple with understanding an American identity.

That understanding must first consider that a true American identity is just one's citizenship or nation of residency. It must decidedly reject any notion of worthiness and embrace this nation's promise of social mobility and diversity. My mom says, "I would leave out being an American first. I think that people need to learn about other cultures…There are great opportunities here for people to reinvent their lives and build their lives from scratch and people that come here from other countries work hard to do that. I think there needs to be more respect [for immigrants]. They're just trying to make a better life."

As a nation, we must embrace immigrants and support their process of situating themselves in our American landscape.

Continuing to ensure that immigrants are granted fair access into our country should be a priority. Vote for and support fair legislation like the Deferred Action for Childhood Arrivals Act (DACA) and other attempts for immigration reform that side with immigrants and their families.

Organizations like Make the Road NY works toward empowering immigrant and working-class communities in New York City. By raising awareness, lobbying, and educating, they are working to tackle discrimination within their communities while also encouraging community organizing.[15]

Normalize the immigrant experience. Shows like *Superstore*, *Fresh Off the Boat*, and *Jane the Virgin* are working to do just that. Media is a powerful agent for change and representation matters. Get to know the cultures of others. De-stigmatize non-native English speakers.

The archaic American identity is being disrupted by tides of black and brown faces, and whether they were born here or not, we should get used to that.

DIY

What is a change that you want to see in the world?

RANDI BROADWELL

"The purpose of life is to live it, to taste experience to the utmost, to reach out eagerly and without fear for newer and richer experience."
~ Eleanor Roosevelt

Who am I?

I was born and raised a small-town girl from Upstate New York with large ambitions. I want to live a life that will allow me to impact and help people. From this burning desire, my interest in the STEM fields has fueled my passion to be a doctor and impact healthcare.

What does changemaker mean to you?

A changemaker is someone who can impact lives in a way that will shift the norm from a low equilibrium to a higher equilibrium. It does not have to be a large change, but in time it could scale up.

What world do I want to live in?

I want to live in a world where happiness is the ultimate goal, a world in which people will not live in the shadow of fear, in which they can be truly who they are. If confidence could be instilled into our children, then they will not face a challenge with apprehension, but as an opportunity to grow.

In order to initiate change, we have to be willing to get uncomfortable.

What characteristic do you love about yourself?

I think it is important to love yourself in your entirety. Your greatest flaws can ultimately be your greatest strengths, but understanding yourself means that you know how to use those characteristics to your advantage. Love to learn and learn to love.

Wanting the Cake and Eating it Too

Randi Broadwell

Introduction: My Story

Randi. Spelled with an 'i' makes it clear that I am female. However, when spoken, the name could also be taken as male. From a young age, I always had stereotypical male and female personality traits. I was a determined, ambitious, and strong minded.

I remember a story my mother recounted about my four-year-old self. I always wanted to go to school with my two older siblings even though I was very little. Since I was an October baby in New York State, I had the opportunity to go to school when I was four or five. Essentially, I had the chance to choose between being the oldest or the youngest in my class. My mother was worried about sending me to school early. However, my young self made very clear to my mother, "I would have killed her if she didn't let me go to school." This was a common theme in my life. I never allowed my mother to dress me, and I insisted I had to do *everything* by myself. I was an unruly little girl. I was aggressive, determined, and loud. All. The. Time.

My parents raised me with gentle guidance in order to grow into the person *I* wanted to be, not into the woman *they* wanted. They raised us all with strict fairness. I suppose they had to given that there were four of us in five years. The boys were the bookends for my sister and I. We were all treated equally. If we wanted something, we had to work for it, including our grades and extracurriculars. Their parenting philosophy taught me work ethic, but most importantly, it taught me to know when I deserved praise. And I realize now that it made us drive ourselves rather than be motivated by external forces. We did what made us happy because that is what my mother's goal for us was, as she told me years later.

Growing up, I never knew about the separation between men and women, boys and girls. My older brother and I constantly played soccer. Since I did not have a travel team to play on, my mother had me attend my brothers' practices, even though the boys were three years older. All I saw was a boy who I was playing soccer against. He was the obstacle in my way of scoring a goal. I never saw myself as weaker or slower because I was a girl. I did not play ball "like a girl." All I saw was a soccer field with freshly painted white lines, sturdy goal posts, and the smell of fresh cut grass.

Isn't that the beauty of childhood innocence? Children do not know stigmas or limits until society tells them that they exist. For example, my younger brother hated the feeling of having his chest exposed when he went swimming. He loved my one-piece swimsuit because it had a dog printed on the front. So my Mom let him wear it...and people thought it was strange because it defied gender roles. She would get strange stares and questions like, "How could you let your son wear a girl's swimsuit?" Her answer was firm: "Because it makes him happy!"

The same idea can be applied to women. Why tell them from a young age that it is wrong to express themselves a certain way? Is it fair to put personality traits on females, such as sweet innocence or willful passivity? Having gone through a traditional school system, boys would often say I was aggressive or intimidating, mainly because I stood up to them. I am forever thankful that my parents raised me to see gender equality by showing me that I can compete with boys. They taught me that when I put in the hard work, I deserve all the glory that comes with it. I should never be ashamed or shy because I am a girl.

What is a Woman To Me?

A woman, what is that? Some might answer *female, wife, mother, sister, daughter, lady,* and *lover*. What are characteristics of women? Again, the typical answers are *beautiful, nurturing, empathetic, caring, agreeable,* and *tolerant*. When a woman moves or acts outside the boundaries of these characteristics, she is often identified as intimidating, bossy, overbearing, rude, and disagreeable. These latter traits have all been used to describe me at some point in my life. But to me, a woman is whatever she wants to be. I am a non-conforming woman who does not fit the traditional role. I am what I think of as an 'unruly woman.'

The characteristics of an 'unruly woman' are usually associated with men. Jordan Peterson points out that the paradox is that 'manly' characteristics are necessary for women to be successful. Agreeable people get paid less than disagreeable people. Women on average are more agreeable than men.[16] Disagreeable is defined by characteristics like being strong-minded, opinionated, intimidating, and loud. Disagreeable is considered a masculine trait; when a woman has this trait, it makes employees less likely to want to work for her. Women will then "back down when they need to sit at the table."[17] The issue is clear; women systematically underestimate their abilities compared to men. Women do not want to be seen as over-confident. Women often do not negotiate for themselves in the workforce. Men attribute their success to themselves, and women attribute theirs to external factors. No one gets a promotion if they do not think that they did it themselves.[18]

Family vs. Career

While there are many factors that contribute to the stigma surrounding the unruly woman, there is still pressure on women to succeed, to bear children, and not to be disagreeable. This tends to put an enormous strain on women today. Women more often face difficult life choices than men. For instance, they are more burdened by the decision to bear children and pursue careers. The idea that they have to choose one or the other, that having both is not feasible, still persists today. By the age of 35, society dictates that women need to have major life events (marriage, family, and career) completed.[19]

Gender equality is still grappling with what society deems "important." For instance, there is still enormous pressure on boys to succeed, but not on girls.[20] There is an emphasis for girls to have families, but not for boys. Therefore, maternity leave in the U.S., on average, is not prioritized in the workforce and can be a source of stress. The United States is one of eight countries, and the only high-income country, as classified by the World Bank, that does not have paid maternity leave. And far fewer countries have paid paternity leave.[21]

The stress of leaving a career or not having sufficient time to promote proper mother and child bonding, forces many new mothers to make an impossible decision. Having to choose a shorter maternity leave entails sacrificing time to bond with the child, but a longer maternity leave forces women to sacrifice their career. Young women today still have to balance the strain of a career and a family, leaving many to choose one over the other.

The Consequence

As the world is changing, the United Nations has recognized gender equality as one of its goals: achieve gender equality and empower all women and girls to know their worth. My childhood has given me the solid foundation to realize that confidence in women is not only needed all over the world, but in our backyards as well. You do not need to look far in order to elicit change. By empowering each other, girls and young women will gain the confidence and experience to advocate for what they want and deserve.

If we can encourage more women to follow their happiness instead of societal expectations, the more likely we will be able to create a sustainable, peaceful, and genuine world. Women can have the power to promote better relationships and end those that are toxic to themselves and others. The idea behind this is simple: women will have the confidence, tools, and mindset to know that they deserve better. However, this is not always possible because of the strain on the gender roles we are constantly asked to follow. It seems as if women have to fight extra hard and ultimately pick and choose what is important to them. They must fight a battle that many men will never have to endure.

Where to Start

The solution to gender inequality has to be a multifaceted approach using sociology, psychology, and biology to our advantage. Who we are is the combination of our minds, bodies, and the societies in which we live. If we could reproduce this biopsychosocial approach that is widely used in medicine today to fit other institutions, it could generate more widespread change. I am not saying: burn the place down and rebuild it, but I am talking about shifting our perspectives and mindsets.

We can start with children when they are young. Give your child room to grow into who they are or wish to be. Send them to school, to schools that teach women about their bodies, personalities, schools that cultivate their personal strengths, support their intellectual and personal growth into unique, individual selves. I know I would have benefited much from such a system. I would not have struggled as much and had a better understanding of who I was. More importantly, I would have been told that it is okay to be different.

The change I envision can not be affected by a singular class, but by daily lessons incorporated into all facets of education, from K-12 and beyond. I did not learn these lessons until I went to college. By talking with students and taking classes with students and professors of different backgrounds, mindsets and agendas, I have learned more about myself as a woman with a non-stereotypical personality.

It is imperative that we give girls the tools to advocate for themselves. Let them become strong and independent. Had I been taught early on to act this way, I could have used my strength to my advantage instead of remaining confused and isolated.

The world's population is composed of half females and half males. While the numbers may be equal, the rights and opportunities are not. If we want to make change in a large part of our population, this is the best place to start. With our girls. Raise them to believe they can succeed and that they deserve equal opportunities. Let them know that they can have the cake and eat it too.

Let's keep women in the workforce in order to move them into executive positions instead of accepting sacrificing their career for their children. How do we make this happen? The answer is not cut and dry; in fact, there will have to be many radical changes in order to find a solution. People will have to put their heads together to figure out how to make this change. How else can we empower others? The answer may be found in our future generations. We need to hold each other accountable in order to find a workable solution.

In our current society, for a woman to get to the top, she has to compete against men. In order for her to succeed, she has to have disagreeable characteristics. An agreeable woman needs to learn how to say "no" and not get pushed around. Therefore, be smart, be conscientious, and be tough. Be an unruly woman. As Sheryl Sandberg stated, "We want women to succeed and be liked for their accomplishments."[22]

Concluding Remarks

Ideas are contagious; they start as a seed that can shift and change into many different shapes and forms. This is the beauty about people with passion. If by reading this story it can change the thinking of one girl, and that one girl spreads this idea to other girls, then the net has been cast, and the domino effect begins. All of this, to become who we want to be by following our passions, will allow for happiness. Let happiness be the motivator of our society and culture, not money. Be nonjudgemental; learn how to listen, but also speak up for yourself.

HANA BROWN

*"All Who Joy Would Win Must Share It.
Happiness Was Born A Twin."*
~ Lord Byron

Who am I?

My name is Hana and I am a 21 years old. I was born in Hawaii, but I grew up in Northampton Massachusetts. I am half Japanese, half White and was raised in a bilingual household. I am a college sophomore at Union College, with a major in Psychology. As hobbies I love jazz music and working with children. I also love sunflowers, the moon, big dogs, and red wine.

What does changemaker mean to me?

To me, a changemaker is someone who puts in the effort to make a difference. They see a problem and they fix it. Whether it be something local or global, it's the people who put their energy in trying to fix an issue, that are making a difference. I think it is very easy to say you will make a change, but actually taking action is much harder.

What world do I want to live in?

I want to live in a world with open dialogue, with candid conversations where both sides are heard and respected even in disagreement. Change in a problem can only start once you are able to understand the needs and concerns of another. Without conversation people will remain in their own bubble not actually connecting to anyone. Change starts with a connection.

What quality would you like to change about yourself?

I hope that one day I can actually make an impact. And, to do that, I think I need to start committing myself more deeply to the things I feel passionate about. There have been too many times in my life where I just think about how I want to get involved. I don't actually commit myself. If it moves me, I should honor that feeling and take action in some way. I believe I am still afraid to take big risks. I fully believe that right now is the time for me to take big risks and make stupid mistakes. So, I wish for my future, that I become even 2% less cautious.

Conversations with a Goat Girl

Hana Brown

She was known as George the Goat Girl, and in just a couple of summers she would make me a better person.

The summer of 2015 was the first time I met George. I had just know her previously as a weird kid with a LOT of goat paraphernalia; pretty much all of her clothes had a goat on it. She was infamous for scolding the farm instructor for not being more knowledgeable about goats, and she would host her own classes on them instead. At the age of 12 she had more vision for her life than I currently hold at 21. She was the first kid to actually sit down and make me listen.

Adults are constantly lying to children, saying it's for their own good. It's never intended to be harmful, just little white lies like Santa Claus or the Tooth Fairy. I've done it too; one time I told kids that snapping turtles can't bite underwater so that they would go swimming in a lake.

It's done to preserve their childhood, to protect them from the big scary adult world. To some extent, it might be necessary, but I also believe that all too often the concerns of kids are overlooked and not heard.

We do not take kids seriously because we are older, wiser and know so much more about the world. It took meeting George for me to fully realize that their world should also have a voice. That their life is just as impacted by the world as mine. But unlike an adult, they are shielded from information and forced to gather it on their own, though sometimes it is inaccurate. The solution is simple: have an open conversation.

George was, and honestly still is the most high strung and interesting kid I have ever met. Her passions include goats, Bernie Sanders, horses, and The New York Times. She was more up to date on politics than I ever will be, and she had hard opinions on them. George was the kind of smart kid that typically would be picked on and isolated when paired with her complete lack of interest in preteen social norms.

While George was awkward, she was also incredibly kind and mature. Although I don't think she ever grasped the love drama and fashion frenzy that others around her were experiencing, she was a good listener. She was patient in listening to everyone in the cabin. It was sometimes easy to forget that she was only twelve. While very intelligent, she still wasn't an adult who could make her own decisions or choices.

That summer, George joined the camp newspaper called *The Firefly*. Most kids wrote about favorite ice cream flavors or camp secrets, but George had more serious issues to address. She wanted to write on gun control and the political right. She wanted to turn it into a negative op-ed piece. I immediately shut down her suggestion. To me it seemed obvious why I could not let her publish that article. It was a large camp with girls as young as seven, and her article could ostracize and offend people.

But George wanted to publish and took my rejection very personally. It was her right to do so, and by asking her to change to a more neutral stance, I was limiting her right to freedom of speech. I was censoring her. Yes, I was the adult who was not taking her seriously.

We argued for weeks, and she was incredibly frustrated with me and the rest of the staff who wouldn't let her publish. She would ignore me. She wouldn't want to hear another perspective. She was so upset that she even cried. And that's when I knew I had to let her voice her opinion, in one way or another.

I asked George why this meant so much to her. She told me about how her family who, while supportive, would never let her be too radical. And how in school she didn't feel accepted enough to be so forthcoming with her ideas. She wanted to talk about it at camp where she was surrounded by people she liked and felt supported. She wanted to spread her passion and involve other kids.

It broke my heart to hear this and know that I had become just another limitation. I made her feel upset and unwelcome. Because she was still just a kid, she had no say, and here, again, adults weren't taking her seriously. Her explanation made me change my mind. Now I also wanted to get her ideas published. I agreed with her stance, but there was just one problem: I was under direct orders from my boss not to let her publish without revisions, because her stance would target other campers and make them feel unwelcome. My hands were tied.

It seems now that my summer experience was a foreshadowing. In February of 2018, a shooting happened at Stoneman Douglas High School in Florida. In it 17 people, 14 students, and 3 faculty were shot and wounded making it one of the most fatal school shootings to date. It was a traumatic event that sparked controversy nationwide, leading to protests, mainly spearheaded by the youth of America.

One of the leaders of this conversation was Emma Gonzalez, a survivor of the shooting.[23] At 19, she is now leading the national conversation on America's gun policy. Nationwide she is empowering kids to take a stance and voice their opinions. To organize protests, and walkouts. She is inspiring young and otherwise powerless people to try and make a change in a government; yet most of them can't even vote. She is an example of how to develop a voice, and she shows that although she is young, she should not be without a say in what world she has to live.

Emma is an inspiration of who I want to be. She is taking a stance and is promoting open conversations. She is a changemaker who is making a difference, her main assets being her passion and her voice. She is a prime example of how a simple conversation can make a world of a difference.

I believe that conversation is the way to making a difference without having to resort to physical means. So, since my summer with George, I've been working hard to have as many open conversations as I can. I like to think that I speak honestly, and I try to listen just as much as I talk.

At camp one of the biggest changes I made was by creating a "Question Jar." I decorated a small jar that I left outside of my door so that kids could anonymously leave a note. The aim was to be able to give my kids the opportunity to ask me about anything that they wanted to know, even if they were too embarrassed to ask me in person. From this I spearheaded a lot of conversations. I talked about periods, sex, politics, sexuality, and less serious things like life in high school and the Kardashians. I learned just as much as I preached. And they are conversations I still remember to this day.

As for George, I eventually got her the right to host weekly forums and discuss with anyone who was interested in attending. It actually turned into a huge hit. The first one was of course gun control, but she then went on to talk about sexuality, institutionalized racism, and political predictions for the fall. As a highly intelligent, kind and caring individual, I learned from her tremendously that summer.

I am aware that it is a parent's choice to decide how much information a child should know about sensitive topics. However, it is naive to think that a child will grow up and not hear about these subjects elsewhere. What is more than likely to happen is that the child will hear wrong information and form opinions on subjects they know little about. This can lead to insensitive or even derogatory ideology, while it really is just a lack of communication. If that is the case, would it not be better to make sure your child is facing life with the most well-balanced and accurate of information?

I think the best way is through open conversation. To take space and make space, listen just as much as you contribute. An open dialogue can lead to major change, as Emma Gonzalez demonstrates. The path to change does not need to be violent, and the very first step is to talk. I will continue to have open conversations with adults and especially kids, to do my part in making sure the world is as fair as it can be.

The summer of 2015 is when I met George. And she was only 12 but had the mind and the heart to take on the world. I want to one day be half as passionate as she was, and along the way support those who have that vision. Meeting George made me a better leader, a better listener, and overall a better person. I will always be thankful that I stopped to really have a conversation with a Goat Girl.

MEGAN BROWN

"Lead, follow, or get out of the way"
~ *my dad, James Brown*

Who am I?

My name is Megan Brown, b. 1998, Union College class of 2021. I am a daughter, I am a sister, I am a student, I am someone who is eager to leave a legacy on the world. I came to Union to gain knowledge and experience to prepare me for an impactful job. I am working towards a career in English and Political Science, with a minor in Spanish, because some of my favorite things to do are write, read, speak, and listen. They are my best skills, and my favorite skills, and I plan to use them to make an impact on issues that I am particularly passionate about.

What does changemaker mean to you?

To be a changemaker means to use your knowledge, passions, and experiences to positively influence an area that you believe could use improvement. True changemakers aren't afraid to get out of their comfort zone or be judged by others, and certainly won't take no for an answer. For true change to happen, persistency, passion, and practice is key.

What world do I want to live in?

I want to live in a world that demonstrates equality, sustainability, and a strong, supporting economy for my children and grandchildren. The generation I am in must be thinking about the future – we must set long-term goals. I want to see more women on the train going to work in New York City and more dads driving the kids around. I want the arbitrary snow days in April to be truly "arbitrary." I want the upper class to follow up on the fact that they say they will "support" the ones that struggle by validating it financially. The world I aspire to not only live in, but also thrive in, is decently different than our world right now. The ideas are there. The resources are there. The changemakers are there. We just have to act.

If you could choose any changemaker to be your mentor, who would it be?

If I could choose any changemaker to be my mentor, I would absolutely choose Martin Luther King Jr. He has always been someone I deeply admire and strive to be like. He met all the qualities, to my standards, of a true changemaker: he had the passion for civil rights, the persistency to continue standing up regardless of the dangers and the rejection, and he practiced what he preached. His "Letter From Birmingham Jail" is definitely one of my favorite works of not only history, but also change – his techniques and rhetoric were so powerful that they are still used today. He was brilliant and certainly carried out his quote, "Our lives begin to end the day we become silent about things that matter."

Who Said It Was "Daddy's Money?"

Megan Brown

It was always easy to point out my parent in the giant crowd at my games and recitals because mine was male. Every time I go to a restaurant with my family, the waiter or waitress hands my dad the check. Then they proceed to thank my dad when we head out the door. If you're looking for a way to piss off my mom, just assume that my dad is the breadwinner.

My town is your standard, affluent, suburban neighborhood, one hour north of Manhattan. All the dads travel to the city to work, while the moms stay home and chauffeur the kids around to their activities. Where I come from, in particular, exemplifies the gender-role stereotype to no end - so much so that Netflix created a show about it: American Housewife. The name itself rings "stay-at-home-mom" while dad is at work all day.

However, this does not apply to my household. I grew up with a dad that works from home while my mom's job is located in the city. My dad was usually one of, if not the only dad in the audience, at my concerts, on the sidelines at my games, and the chaperone on my field trips. My mom came as often as she could, and was there for the most crucial moments. Nevertheless, I felt awkward. I felt different. Why was he the only dad in the audience? This question was constantly circling around my seven-year-old mind, until I got older and realized that we, even in 2018, are living in a male-dominated society. We still live in a society that has distinct perceptions of the roles women should play, and those of men. I aspire to influence change in these perceptions by using the experience I have gained in my household, my town, and at my job.

Because my entire childhood seemed, and was, an anomaly, I decided to look for answers. The preconceived notions of gender roles develop at a younger age than some might think. One study found that, "Girls did two more hours of chores a week while boys got twice as much time to play. This dynamic carries a lesson for both genders: girls learn that housework falls on their shoulders, and boys learn that girls will clean up after them."[24] This dynamic is a snowball effect of stereotypical beliefs spreading down from generation to generation.

Another study in *The Nation* showed that, "Even mothers who work full-time will still put in a week and a half's worth more time on household tasks than their male partners each year."[25] Though statistics show that there is an increasing number of women that work full-time, the advancement of technology makes it easier to display these stereotypes in the media for everyone, including today's children, to watch.

One of the most common means of gender stereotyping is through TV commercials. Marketing messages illustrate the point: "only about 2 percent of commercials featuring men show them cooking, cleaning or running after kids, while the majority of commercials featuring women are selling home products like cleaners or furniture."[26] How can the next generation of media producers change the way gender roles are portrayed? What could a shift in messaging mean for the life choices of the next generation of girls and boys?

The past few summers I have been working at a local racquet club, where I get the rewarding experience of working with both kids and adults. Most of my experiences there have been wonderful, however, I have certainly run into sexist instances. Every once and while, the club hosts member-guest round-robin doubles tournaments and I was sometimes asked to fill in.

Now, typically this isn't a problem. All of the members are friendly and inclusive, including the men, however this particular time was not so amiable. I was assigned by my boss to be partners with a man and this particular player was not pleased, to say the least. Now, I doubt the animosity was a result of my age, considering my title "Junior Pro" has more than enough experience and ability in its name. I was the only young woman in this tournament, and this man did not make me feel good about it. Not only did he hardly speak to me the entire tournament, but he rolled his eyes when I missed a shot, and he even made sure to cover as much court as he could, - quite "ball-hog ." This experience reinforced my dedication to gender equality.

Women are allowed to be confident. They should be confident. They have much to offer the world. But, oftentimes society perceives men and women who are confident in different ways. For instance, women run three of the top 25 newspaper titles in the U.S. and only one of the top 25 titles in the world. That number has decreased in the past 10 years, according to Griffin's research. Jill Abramson was the first female executive editor at *The New York Times,* yet her tenure in that position lasted fewer than three years. Fired in May 2014, Abramson said that although gender was not the main reason for her departure from the Times, it played a role: "I think I was judged unfairly by a double standard tied to gender at the Times...The higher women go, the more disliked they are, which is not true for men."[27] Abramson hired a lawyer in 2014 to investigate the pay gap between her and a male predecessor, earning her the label "pushy" from the Times' top management. It is often noticed that when women are granted top executive roles and do their best to drive the company forward, they are seen as "bitchy" or "condescending." However, when men fill the same role, and take the same progressing actions, they are admired for their dedication and determination to bring success to the business.

After researching the root of this gender disparity, I began thinking: is this an issue of nature or nurture? I've realized that it's absolutely a combination. However, at an early, impressionable age, it starts with nurture. Kids observe the roles and responsibilities of those who they live with, and subconsciously act them out as soon as they can. Psychologist Lev Vygotsky found that, "Imitation and instruction are vital components to children's development. Adults promote this learning by role-modeling behavior, assisting with challenging tasks, and passing along cultural meanings to objects and events, all of which are components of gender development."[28] Playing "house" is a perfect example of how children also emulate what goes on in their own home. These behaviors are then enabled by toys like Fisher Price kitchens and houses - precisely directed towards the *typical little girl*.

Like "house," gender-based messages found on most everyday items (towels, blankets, toys, supplies), not to speak of clothing, will inevitably overpower even the most well-meaning parents in terms of exposure to gender segregation. Think about it: "If aisles were thus segregated by race, most people today would be appalled, and yet it is considered normal where gender stereotypes are concerned. Fortunately, activists, consumer groups and concerned parents are starting to react to this, demanding an ending to gender segregation in the marketing of children's toys – see for instance the *Lettoysbetoys* and *PinkStinks* campaigns promoted in UK."[29]

Gender stereotyping goes both ways. Gloria Steinem said one of my favorite quotes to this day: "We've begun to raise daughters more like sons... but few have the courage to raise our sons more like our daughters." The emphasis that people put on achieving "masculinity," in my opinion, is way too large. We must flip this habit if we want to start to see gender perception equalize. We must break the cycle by asking our boys to do the dishes and telling our girls to go out and play ball.

The perception of women in society needs to change. It is harming the confidence of girls and women in all of our communities. I greatly value my childhood and the fact that I grew up in a very different household. Although I have always envied the kids who got to bring their moms to chaperone field trips, my dad has been a solid replacement, even if the other kids and moms regarded him with amazement. My experience growing up in a home free of stereotypical gender roles has ignited my passion to not be limited in any way by my gender.

My house shouts women empowerment. I will use what I've been accustomed to at home to fulfill my ambitions and dreams, and to inspire girls and women now and in the next generation. I hope to inspire my own daughters, granddaughters, and nieces to continue a family tradition of independence. I want to make my parents proud, follow in my mom's footsteps, and eliminate any possibility of any woman having an asterisk next to their successes: that they were good "for a girl."

If you're looking for a way to achieve gender equality, don't assume the dad is the breadwinner. Although society is still portraying women in stereotypical ways, supporting diverse female and male roles in our home and work environments will begin to change our world. The next generation can break the mold and stop seeing the world through "daddy's money."

DIY

If you could choose any changemaker to be your mentor, who would it be and why?

KAITLYN CONNOR

"He quickly saw that these people would believe anything that was shouted at them loudly and convincingly enough."

~ *George S. Schuyler, Black No More*

Who am I?

My name is Kaitlyn Connor, I am a 19 year-old first year at Union College. I am originally from Farmingville, NY. I enjoy reading and spending time with friends. A fun fact about myself is that I'm in an accelerated law program at Union.

On the surface it's easy to see: I'm a daughter, a sister, a student, a friend, among many other roles I play in my life. However, there is something more. I'm an ambitious and dedicated young woman with a goal to make a difference. I grew up in middle class Long Island in a perfectly average family in a perfectly average home. However, I always wanted something more, my goal is to increase equality globally and support those who want to do so. I am strength and independence and creativity. I am a millennial.

What type of world do I want to live in?

People tend to be incredibly selfish; it is an innate response in such a competitive society. However, why does it always have to be this struggle to see who can come up on top? Most are so focused on trying to make sure they aren't the ones being taken advantage of, that people stop caring about others. My goal for the perfect world would be for all to put others first above themselves and accept the diversity that creates the originality within ourselves that we all thrive in.

What does changemaker mean to you?

The term changemaker may seem very daunting to most people. However, it doesn't have to be. We can all find something that we are passionate about, but what separates a changemaker is an *intense* ambition and passion applied to a cause that you truly care about. Being a changemaker at its core means seeing a problem in our society and knowing you need to make a difference. Once you can find something you are passionate about and genuinely want to make a difference, you too can be a changemaker.

Why is social change such an important issue?

Even in 2018 we still deal with some of the same issues we've been attempting to solve for decades. Clearly, there is something wrong with the way in which issues like immigration and gender discri-mination is being addressed worldwide. Many are crying for social help. The real question is: will we be the generation to make a difference?

No Child Left Behind, Except You, You and You

Kaitlyn Connor

My father was left behind. His whole life he was left behind, told by numerous teachers and adults that he was worthless and wouldn't amount to much. He nearly failed high school; his degree depended on one teacher's generosity with a test score. Bouncing around from college to college, dropping out and re-enrolling…. maybe they were right.

My dad didn't think so. By working his ass off he struggled through many years of schooling and jobs that didn't quite fit him. Today he stands as the "boss" at a bustling business. As a child you would've never guessed this would be his future. Since he was struggling with undiagnosed ADD his whole life, he did poorly in school. Yet, he had an above average IQ. Ironically, even as an extremely intelligent man, he had trouble focusing, resulting in poor grades. Trapped by a system that worked against him, my Dad "fell behind" due to his learning disability. Many children had stories like this. However, the world saw an issue, and the world did something about it.

Growing up in New York State there has always been a strong emphasis on the "No Child Left Behind"act. In the past, many children in the public school systems were overlooked. Many had undiagnosed learning disabilities and were often left behind their classmates and not given an equal chance to succeed. In such a competitive world as today, to get jobs that used to be way more attainable, "No

Child Left Behind" seemed like a great system to make sure that kids who struggle don't have their futures impeded.

As a child, I can remember kids being pulled from classes for help in speech or writing, or getting extra time on tests. Acts such as these truly helped kids keep up in a fast-paced learning environment meant to challenge students and create stronger candidates for college. However, despite these supports, there is a new call that needs to be addressed for the next generation: children with more severe disabilities in New York have frequent educational and budget gaps and get the least amount of resources readily available when, ironically, they need it the most.[30]

I was fortunate enough to be offered inside access into what much of the general population can't, or doesn't care to see. My mom has been a social worker for Suffolk County Early Interventions nearly my entire life. Early Intervention is a state sponsored program that treats babies born with disabilities ranging from cerebral palsy to a speech developmental delay.[31] People like my mother would assess the children and if they were deemed appropriate for treatment, there were meetings set up with whomever was needed for that child's particular case. It was always a highlight of my week when I would tag along with my mom to her job, when I would get to participate in this ever stimulating environment and, most importantly of course, get to play with all the babies that were brought to the meetings.

As I matured I was able to appreciate all that my brother, my friends and I had been fortunate enough to grow up with. Seeing that not everyone had the same advantages as we did, made me realize that this was something I wanted to learn more about. Originally, I asked my mom to show me more about how her meetings and the therapy sessions worked. With the gracious participation of the staff of Early Interventions I was able to get a behind-the-scenes look and truly comprehend what it means to have a birth defect or disability. I learned how this affects a child growing up and the best ways to live a fulfilling life.

I was very interested and sympathetic in all that I had been lucky enough to witness; nonetheless, I wasn't really able to relate much to these children. I was a teenage girl and these were babies and toddlers. But then I started to wonder, what happens when kids age out of Early Intervention? I asked my mom, and she led me to a school called UCP, or United Cerebral Palsy Center, which would go on to change my life.

UCP is an institution dedicated to educating youth ages five to twenty-one with disabilities in a sensory safe environment. Early Interventions often recommended kids that they had worked with to this school and schools like this after they aged out of the program so they could continue on with their education.[32] When I was sixteen I visited it for the first time with my mother.

Upon visiting UCP, I realized what a profound impact it had, and I had to be a part of it. Our society often forgets about children like this. There is such a big focus on aiding children with learning disabilities or minor delays that we often overlook children with more severe issues. The common attitude seems to be that it's someone else's problem, or it appears as a hopeless cause. Nevertheless, all the children in the educational system should be treated equally and given equivalent resources to fit their needs. Visiting this school even the first time, showed me a whole new world I had never really thought about.

Over 13% of all children enrolled in the public schooling system have a severe disability.[33] That's over 6 million children, yet this fact still seems to be brushed aside frequently. Something incredible that I experienced was being exposed to an insanely dedicated staff and hardworking students. I had always thought I took my education very seriously, but seeing the students and staff at UCP, I realized many others have to work much harder than I ever did. Why then do they not get the same privileges as I do?

During my time at UCP I was able to meet some of the hard working staff, including Jennifer Adelson and Virginia Castanga. People such as Jen and Virginia have dedicated their lives and careers to helping improve these children's lives. But before we can figure out how to improve UCP, we must first understand how it all works.

The program begins with Early Intervention, as I mentioned previously. Beginning therapy as young as possible is most effective. This will of course help the child understand their disability, but it will also help them feel comfortable with therapy sessions and new people. At such a young age, it is crucial that this is established quickly. Toddlers tend to be weary of strangers and new situations, making future therapy more difficult for adjustment if it is not started earlier.[34]

Once a child ages out at age three, they are given the advice to further their therapy, now combined with an educational factor at schools such as UCP. After pre-school, classes are offered for ages five through twenty-one for children who qualify for specialized services that their school districts can't offer.[35]

In recent years support for children with severe disabilities has become an upcoming issue, with organizations such as UCP making sure these kids aren't "left behind" like so many in the past. UCP goes above and beyond trying to give the best experience and education possible to these children. And it boasts, along with many other schools like it, ungraded classes with a high teacher to student ratio, frequent clinical services, art and music programs, and parents and community partnerships to play an active role in their education.[36]

Additionally, it has been discovered that sensory learning plays a big role in the success of the programs at UCP. During my many visits, I witnessed several lessons, almost all involving sensory stimulation. In particular there seemed to be a heavy emphasis on technology, which is clearly an upcoming field. We can attribute many of the improvements in the education systems of children with disabilities to the 1990 World Conference, which brought the world's attention to something it had for so long neglected.[37] Despite recent improvements, there are still changes to be made.

More funding and attention needs to be given to schools. If schools like UCP had more funding, the progress they could make could change lives of students and families. It seems obvious that more schools like this should exist and get more attention, so why haven't they? America tends to avoid addressing things that make us uncomfortable. No one wants to admit that situations like these are neglected, but that is our reality and change needs to be made.

I made a change. When I was sixteen years old I watched these students thrive in an environment that catered to their needs, and it was amazing. However, I still see now what I saw then: a severe lack of attention and empathy, and I wanted to change that. Compliant with the educational benefit of sensory learning I decided to build a musical interactive garden within which the children could have lessons. This was a huge undertaking, but I knew I had to play my part. With the help of friends and family, I raised over $900 to buy and build decking and planters that could be wheelchair accessible.

While putting in the planters and musical components, I felt as though my action, despite being small in the grand scheme of things, could actually make a difference in these families' lives. The most fulfilling part of the project was when it was completed and I watched everyone use the planters and enjoy themselves. Maybe it didn't mean much overall, but it meant something to them and it meant something to me.

There's still an enormous issue to be addressed with the neglect of these schools and the children that attend them, but getting a community to pay attention is the first step to a more national acknowledgment.

As Millennials, we are all so young and the possibility of making any real change seems impossible. Maybe that's true. After all, don't many of the dreams we chase often involve much bigger players than we could ever be? We should never stop trying, we are the future and it is our job to be the change that we aspire to create.

There is no telling what your own actions can do for someone else. What may seem small and insignificant to you could change someone's life. I saw a change I wanted to make and I did something about. There are still many problems that need to be addressed in this field, and that's okay. I made a change in my community, brought attention to an overlooked problem, and made a difference in those kids' lives. In the future, there needs to be reforms, children with severe disabilities can't be continuously overlooked. Schools like UCP are doing a phenomenal job in providing education, but they need more support from our communities and our governments. As a nation, we need to truly stick by our claim, and leave no child behind.

SASHA CURRIE

"I cried because I had no shoes until I met a man with no feet."
~ Helen Keller

Who am I?

With one look, you wouldn't be able to tell, but Caribbean blood runs through my veins. A daughter of both Haitian and Jamaican parents; encompassed by the same region, yet separated by distinct islands. I'm a college student. I aspire to be many different things, but have yet to choose one. I hope to become a genuinely good person who has a positive effect on the people around me, my community, and society in general.

How do I see myself as a changemaker?

Growing up, I was very different from my peers. We all have these social constructs that limit certain things we do. Many people told me that because I was female I wouldn't be able to practice martial arts. It was seen as a male sport. However, I encouraged my parents to sign me up and later became one of their greatest students. I see myself as a changemaker who continues to break down the barriers that keep me from doing the things I love, especially because I don't have the same opportunity as others to follow my dreams. I hope that by doing this I can influence people in similar situations to not be discouraged by what others may say to bring them down.

What world do I want to live in?

A world where there is less crime is ideally the world I would want to live in. Where I live, most of the issues we face on a daily have to do with crime against neighbors and family members. Also, most conflicts are a result of differences between race, culture, religion, and other issues that shouldn't be fought over. I want to live in a world where individuals don't judge each other, especially based on things they have no control over.

What did our parents think social change was. Do our parents view children as changemakers?

When my parents were about my age, social change to them meant something different than how we view it now. I'm a child of two African American parents. During their time, social change was all about race. Social change meant being able to get along with one another regardless of the color of their skin. It meant to be able to greet and converse with people who were different from them, except where the only difference resided in their complexions.

Now social change means different things. Apart from race it's about environmental struggles, sexual orientation, changes in government policy, etc. There's more variety and room for thought when it comes to the idea of social change.

What does changemaker mean to you?

A changemaker to me is someone who takes charge in any given situation; a leader who not only sees problems in the world but works towards finding solutions to them.

OMG, Please Kill Me Now

Sasha Currie

You see them everyday...
They pass by you. Engage in polite speech.
Act according to what's expected of them in today's society, so you'd never suspect a thing.
You could never figure out what they were hiding. Saying it out loud would be too easy.
It's a game. Their game. And they will always win.
It's your job to uncover the secret, to be observant, to solve the puzzle, the mystery.
What we all seem to forget in these situations is that they desperately want you to.
They can't say it, but they want you to know.
"I don't know how to tell you, but I'm….."
"Can you please help me? I'm..."
"I hope you're not disappointed in me. I'm…"
I'm..
i'M..
I'M SUICIDAL

It's never easy to talk about these issues, especially when societal pressures tell you that this particular matter isn't up for discussion. In the above poem I hoped to capture as accurately as I could, the thoughts and emotions of a person who'd contemplated suicide. Did I do a good job? Or did I fall into the trap of misconceptions; misconceptions commonly associated with individuals who had suffered so badly that the only solution they could think of was to take their own lives. Ask me why I wrote it? Well, would I have been able to capture your attention otherwise? Now that you're here, I have something important to tell you.

First, everything is not going to be okay. And second, suicide is not a game. It's not a mind game, or a puzzle that you can solve. This issue has been over-looked for far too long. Things need to change.

When I engaged in a conversation about suicide prevention with Annika, one of my peers at Union, we began to talk about how on social media and other platforms, suicide is often romanticized for the purpose of pure entertainment. For example, take the Netflix series *13 Reasons Why*. This Netflix series is about a girl who experienced a wide range of horrible things that later influenced her to take her own life. Hannah Baker, the main character, leaves behind a sequence of cassette tapes explaining the "reasons" why she made the "choice" to commit suicide.[38] Annika later suggested that the tapes perpetuate the idea that there's a concrete reason behind someone committing suicide, when in reality, few have concrete "reasons" and not everyone leaves a note behind. The notion that after you've passed you'll be able to punish people for what they've done, getting revenge in a way, is fictitious. This series appeals to people because of the way it portrays suicide, with mysteries and clues that keep the viewers sitting at the edge of their seats, but it doesn't accurately demonstrate the reason why individuals try to commit suicide.

Although the series doesn't portray suicide as it should, Annika and I agreed that it has gotten people talking. It has opened the topic for discussion and that's a start towards making a difference in many people's lives.

Talking with Cynthia, another one of my peers from Union, we reflected on how individuals who commit suicide often have no one to talk to who can truly understand their situations. It makes it that much harder when counselors are there to help, but society generally tells people that seeing a therapist is wrong. Subsequently, they don't end up getting the help they need.

I often wonder why there is a stigma around the concept of going to therapy, counseling, or seeing a psychiatrist? It is because asking for help in today's society is associated with weakness. Parents especially, at times, are afraid of allowing their children to go to counseling. Whenever they hear or see the word psychiatrist, the first thought that comes to mind is that they must be "crazy" or have some sort of "mental illness" that needs to get "fixed."

In our society, individuals behave as if everyone is perfect at handling the struggles of everyday life alone. They also make it seem as if counseling isn't used for other moments in our lives, like asking for another individual's opinion on a topic, an important decision you may have to make in your life, or just for having a support system in your pursuit of a successful future.

Not too long ago, someone very important to me, a woman in my family, attempted suicide. I was raised to believe that going to therapy wasn't necessary. I was taught that going to church every Sunday and praying often would aid me in the problems I encountered in life. So, when I witnessed her parents tell her the same things my parents once told me, I thought everything would eventually be okay. I came to find out it wasn't. Of course, when she survived, her parents were more open to seeking help from counselors. It is wrong that it took her attempted suicide for changes to be made. It shouldn't have come that far. I almost lost her; the one person who understood who I was. I also came to realize that maybe her ability to not judge and treat everyone with such kindness and care, came from her inability to see her own self worth.

At times, religious interference contributes to the confusion or lack of acceptance when it comes to allow-ing children to see a counselor. Families with strong religious backgrounds tend to tell their children that all problems in their lives can be fixed with prayer. If their child comes to them feeling down or depressed, they would tell them to pray and expect the way they're feeling to subside. However, what happens when that child prays and things don't change? What do they do then? Taking action while praying isn't a bad thing. It's important to know that seeking a counselor doesn't mean that you don't believe or lack faith in God. Faith and counseling should not be mutually exclusive. Depression is not a phase, and no one wants to find themselves in a position in which they denied someone support after they are already gone.

Suicidal individuals can sometimes find it difficult to ask for help. Cynthia and I also discussed how these individuals could be closed up to their families, or bottle all of their emotions inside, thinking that letting it all out would result in them being sent to a psych ward. There are parents or caretakers who allow their children to seek help from counselors for being clinically depressed, have other mental illnesses or disorders/diseases, but they don't allow them to be medicated for it. Without a holistic approach to suicide prevention, individuals can find themselves in a circular downward spiral. They may start to do poorly in school or act out in ways they never have before. Not succeeding in life can increasingly contribute to depression, which in turn also contributes to factors that drive individuals to kill themselves.

Depending on where or how you were brought up, your parents might have had specific rules, a common one being that you should always show respect to your elders. In the case where a child might act up, doing something they shouldn't, parents might be quick to punish instead of discussing why they behaved that way. They also might not ask what they can do to help if it was brought on by a major issue a child were to experience in life. In those cases where parents are quick to punish, not listen or try to understand, it makes things harder. When the people who've been with you all your life, who took care of you, and raised you, don't understand or try to understand; when you have no one else to turn to, what do you do?

Suicide is the 10th leading cause of death in the US. Each year 44, 965 people lose their lives to suicide and for every 1 successful suicide there are 25 attempts, according to the American Foundation for Suicide Prevention.[39] What can we do to reduce rates of suicide? What can we do to stop people from feeling like suicide is the only way they can solve their problems?

For one, we can listen and try to understand. It's not easy to comprehend what could drive someone to kill themselves, but listening helps. Another thing we can do is continue to encourage individuals who feel suicidal to seek help from professionals. It's important to make them feel like it's okay to go to therapy as opposed to it meaning there is something wrong with them or that it makes them mentally unstable, or crazy. We need to talk about it to each other and in schools. We shouldn't push it aside and ignore someone who comes to you for help. Letting them know that they aren't alone, making it relatable, and showing empathy goes a long way. We need to convince them that life isn't meaningless and that committing suicide isn't the answer or the key to solving their problems.

GIUSEPPE DE SPUCHES

"Going in one more round when you don't think you can – that's what makes all the difference in your life."

~ *Rocky Balboa*

Who am I?

I am neither Italian nor American, I am somewhere in between. What does "in between" mean? I guess we'll just have to find out.

What world do I want to live In?

I don't believe that there can be one world and that we all live in a similar environment. No matter what happens, at least in my lifetime, there will always be substantial differences between the living conditions in different parts of the world. Ideally, I would want to live in a world in which people can be educated and can understand what is best for themselves and their community, without having to blindly follow a leader. Such a state, which might be a utopia, could yield a global society in which the good of the community would be considered equally as important as the well-being of the individual.

Education is not only important for literacy, but intellectual knowledge is important to understand how people around us think and act, which, in an ideal world, would lead to a better overall understanding of other people, and potentially reduce conflict.

Why is social change such an important issue, especially today having so much information available all the time?

In today's world we have an abundance of information available to us at any time. With a simple click we can literally have access to anything we are interested in. Precisely because we know so much, it is hard to have knowledge and care about everything. There are so many problems in the world that we would lose our mind if we were to try to keep up with all of them.

Social change is important because each individual on this planet has unique skills and knowledge. If we can channel what makes us unique, and be leaders in the areas that we are most familiar with, each one of us can make an impact. We don't all need to hit a home run, we all need to hit singles.

What does changemaker mean to you?

To promote change we need to first be aware of what needs to be changed. We cannot expect to help someone whose shoes we never walked in. In fact, one could argue that western colonization of Africa and Asia is the best example of how the lack of understanding of cultures was detrimental to bringing change to impoverished regions.

To me, changemaker means to care about a specific issue, to truly understand what the problem is. Ideally, one would have to be affected by the matter to really grasp its severity. Once we comprehend what we are dealing with, we can then promote change. Changemaking is about communities coming together to improve their lifestyle - to go from a low level equilibrium, to a high level equilibrium. A changemaker is anyone who is actively involved in this process.

We Don't Need No Education

Giuseppe De Spuches

Victor Hugo, the French romantic poet, once wrote that the role of authors and literates in society could be compared to that of the lighthouse in navigation. They were supposed to guide their fellow citizens through darkness, helping them to understand the world and the problems pleasures of their lives. Similarly, a teacher is supposed to guide students in their first years of life, to help them learn how to face problems, how to think, how to act.

Education is a complicated subject. The reason it is meaningful to me is that although I grew up in one of the wealthiest neighborhoods in one of the wealthiest cities in Italy, with access to some of the (supposed) best educations in the country, I still feel like I was never given real guidance by my teachers as to how to live in this world.

I recognize that it may be hard, as a reader, to listen to a kid who comes from a privileged background complain about how education was not good enough for him. To truly make a difference in someone's life it is important to fully understand their struggle first. How can I understand the struggles of children in poor communities that might not even have water, and who might not even *think* about sitting in a classroom and receiving what us westerners consider an education? What the hell do I know?

I think I can connect with them on a different level: I lacked a proper education because of educators who did not push me to think, did not teach me to be creative or innovative, and did not help me individuate my strengths and weaknesses. Through this experience I understood that without learning, our lives are empty.

We are born without knowledge, and the only way to move forward in life is to discover new skills and master them. This automatically happens at a very young age - we don't just happen to learn how to walk and talk. We observe our parents and the people around us, and we replicate what they do. We are guided. Similarly, all children around the world should be guided through the early stages of life. I believe that we should constantly be learning and adapting. That is our greatest strength as humans.

The Problems We Are Facing

However, over the course of the past decade, the light in our metaphorical lighthouse has been dimming. A common problem in developing a country's school system is the lack of funding for education. As reported by the *Global Citizen* in January of 2018, in the last 9 years there has been a 4% decrease in educational funding in developing nations by nonprofits and private funders. This funding crisis, which coincides with the financial crisis of 2009, has had a strong impact on children's ability to go to school in countries such as Ghana, Kenya and Ethiopia.[40]

One of the reasons for this decline is that higher levels of education have much stronger rates of return. This means that profit is usually higher when funding the education of students in private universities than helping small marginalized communities in poorer countries. However, the ones who need that money the most are the children in poor communities. Like most businesses, profit seems to be overshadowing the good of potential funding, thus emphasizing the need for more funding of education at lower levels. It's an unfair world.

Other factors that have caused a decrease in financial aid in education is the lack of donor coordination, ineffective division of labor, and unpredictable support by donors or agencies. What makes the situation worse is the inefficient or non-existence of data on the progress that schools and children make through the aid of donors.[41] Reports about the effectiveness of bringing education to low income areas have been very inaccurate. This has discouraged donors who don't get to observe the impact they make on marginalized populations.

Many communities across the world don't have teachers, classrooms, or learning materials. Naturally, without these resources it is impossible for anyone to receive an education.[42] The problem is more serious than most people realize. While some locations lack these resources altogether, others do have them available, but they are sub-par, to the point of being equivalent to not having them at all.

Not having a teacher or having one that has never been trained, and possibly even lacks an education of their own, could be considered the same issue. Teaching is a serious matter and whoever takes on a role as an educator must understand that the job is very nuanced. Understanding a child's strengths and weaknesses, knowing their background, what they are exposed to at home, what they are exposed to when they are around other students, what their personality is like… There are many aspects that need to be accounted for, and it is part of the instructor's job to recognize what each child's obstacles will be in learning.

Developing countries are burdened by additional challenges and limitations, especially during natural catastrophes or political events.[43] The impact of these events, which seem to be unrelated to education, limit the growth path of many children who may regularly have to change their lifestyle based on the political or climatic reality of their country or region. Without a stable growth path, with uncertainty and lack of information, it is hard to develop the mind of a child.

These issues barely scratch the surface regarding the problem of lack of education on a global scale, but they seem to be a common cause for the slow and unstable advent of education to the less fortunate corners of the world.

An organization that has been successful in bringing education to the least wealthy communities is *Pencils of Promise*. Adam Braun, the founder, was a young man who believed in the value of education and, through persistence and the building of community buy-in, as well as financial connections, has now built 468 primary schools in Ghana, Guatemala, Laos and Nicaragua. There are about 80 thousand students[44] enrolled in the program, and they have been receiving an education free of worry caused by financing or instability. The schools' objective is to teach children by giving them opportunities and resources to reach their literacy goals.[45] *Pencils of Promise* is training teachers to be educators, but also to serve as role models while providing safe school structures and education about sanitation. Their objective is to create a learning environment that allows their students to stay healthy and stay in school.

Education is the foundation of a country's identity. Education forms the minds of the people who shape that identity, community, demographic, region and values. Without education, how can a country ever progress?

My Story of Change

This is the root of my commitment to education: most people in marginalized and underprivileged countries live in difficult conditions because of political and economic adversities, which are often out of their control. But because they usually lack access to information and the means to better their situation, they are unable to better their lives.

Many years ago, my grandfather, a Union College alumnus, founded a primary school in a small town in India and provided basic medical education to the community of the village where the school was located. He provided children and adults with the basic knowledge that most Europeans or North Americans take for granted.

My American grandfather flew to India on a small and unstable plane. The only thing narrower than the aisle were the seats. Even the mildest turbulence created a hole in every passenger's stomach (and probably the pilot's). Once the aircraft finally landed on the dirt road that was the airport landing strip, my grandfather, Bob, stepped off the plane.

He arrived at a small, rural village in central India, whose name I won't even attempt to write, and onto what an upper-class American family would think of as a stereotypical Indian caravan: a blue bus, with dirty windows and straw baskets tied to the roof with ropes. For locals this was an elite limousine service. The next day, Bob made his way over to the school he had started ten years earlier to meet with the children that were enrolled in the program and with the adults who had been applying modern day medicine to a not-so-modern day society. He was greeted with strong enthusiasm. The adults proudly showed off the facilities, from classrooms to infirmaries, visibly nervous as to whether they had impressed Bob or not. Later, the children even put on a musical act that included dance and costumes.

When the school and medical program were first set up, Bob worked closely with the community; he helped them find a building and furnish it, and he provided funds to start the classes and find basic medicine. After that he wasn't as present; he gave the people of the village space to grow. The most impressive feat the community achieved was gaining enough knowledge of the world to sustain themselves.

Although the westernization of poorer countries is not necessarily an example of positive change, the benefit of knowing about diseases, how they transmit and how they affect the human body was very useful information to the Indian community. Their growth was exponential over the course of those ten years, and it might have even been an anomaly. But, imagine if that growth ratio was sustained over the next twenty years. Where might the village and its children be in two or three decades from now? Although it might be unrealistic to think that this could happen all over the world, the strength of education can help people reach some impressive goals.

The Changemakers' Obstacles

Poverty and a lack of education leads to sub-par living conditions. In fact, a study by the International Monetary Fund has shown that life expectancy is actually lower in countries where information about health and access to quality health care is limited. The most stunning example is in Hungary, where uneducated people on average live 14 years less than their counterparts.[46] Furthermore, poor health leads to disruption in employment and often in family stability, which in turn leads to lower productivity and weaker economies.

Bringing education to children who lack the possibility to go to school has been a goal for many organizations. Like many other challenges in this world, there is no one answer to solve every community's problem. Each country and each region has different obstacles on their path towards literacy. Therefore, it is hard to pinpoint a universal strategy to find a solution because oftentimes it isn't clear to changemakers what issues to tackle to begin with.

Each community has specific issues it needs to address and learn about and that is the call for change that we should all want to be a part of. The reason it is so hard to improve education around the globe is that there is a disproportionate ratio between the people who need help and those who are actually helping them. And because each situation is unique, it is extremely hard for such few people to accurately and successfully make a difference. Each demographic needs attention, and no group can be lumped under a general educational system policy. We cannot fix the world by taking one giant step.

Going to a country, building a school and teaching what we think is right is not a successful strategy to better the lives of those in need. We have to look at it as a process in which each step will be difficult and may not lead to a short term improvement. For example, finding a way to make schools physically accessible to everyone may seem like a waste of time, but it is a crucial stepping stone towards educating our entire population. By taking the time to develop what we take for granted first, like a bed, a breakfast, a bus that takes us to school, a clean building, we can make a true difference in someone's education. As unbelievable as it may sound, many areas in the world need to start from this basic place. Ours included.

DIY

How did your parents view social change?

How do their views differ form yours?
Why do you think that is?

JACQUES PIERRE TREGUIER

Who am I?

I'm half French and half Tibetan. I train for triathlons competitively and have a deep passion for innovation and entrepreneurship. I was originally born in France, but grew up primarily in Colorado. I'm training to be on the starting team for the Olympics in Triathlon.

Why is social change such an important issue, today having so much information available all the time?

We have too much information available to us. This is a good and bad thing. Essentially there is so much information that if left untrained, our minds wander towards material that does not matter and will have little to no positive impact on the world we live in. I struggle with this lack of focus as well. Thus, in order to have the best future we possibly can for future generations, we have to focus now what's objectively important to the survival of our society. If that means changing a lot of our current consumption system to minimize waste and maximize recycling, then we'll take steps to do so. Social change is everything.

What world do I want to live in?

I want to live in a world where the younger generation does not have to fear for their health due to climate change and especially from pollution. The health of our planet is important to me, and I hope to make sure it stays healthy for us to continue living here for many more years. I also love the U.S., in the sense that we have the most freedom of speech and thought. Those are two principles I believe are essential to the development of our society and continued success as a nation.

If you could choose any changemaker to be your mentor, who would it be?

100% Elon Musk. In my opinion he is hands down the greatest entrepreneur of our generation. Although I'm sure he wouldn't have time for me, I think it would be amazing to get more information on his mindset and inner thoughts on how his stress tolerance and work ethic are so consistently high. I'd also love to learn how he manages his time to be so efficient as to manage over three massive companies to great success.

A Solution to Pollution

Jacques Pierre Treguier

I have my purpose set out for me. I want to guarantee the safety of future generations to be able to live optimally on this planet for years and years to come.

I was lucky enough to be born and raised in an environment where the air is not toxic and the water is potable. Food is available along with job opportunities and safety from external threats. I believe it's only right to try to pass that same opportunity, if not a better one, on to the future generations of the world.

I was drawn into this issue during my travels to both Beijing and New Delhi, the capitals of the two countries with the largest populations in the world. I loved my time in both countries, but the physical experience was toxic, literally. When I visited Beijing, it was my first time in China. We landed. I looked outside the oval airplane window and saw what I thought was a heavy fog. I wondered if this was common for the weather. It was not fog. The grey I saw blanketed the entire region, and I came to the realization that it was from heavy pollution.

The pollution in New Delhi was hardly different than in China. I saw litter on the streets and it seemed to be poorly managed. When litter was collected by the city, it was usually burned. This was a major contributor to the smog and toxic air that encapsulated the capital of India.[47]

I would read about this kind of environment emerging as I grew older and decided to see it for myself to better ingrain it into my mind. It helped me remember that outside of the high quality of life enjoyed in the US by most of the population, plenty of other countries needed entrepreneurial engagements to improve their living conditions.

This initially sparked curiosity within me. The curiosity I found would undergo change. It transformed into disappointment with our current systems. This would lead to anger as I continued to read material online about negative externalities from human consumption. What could we do besides burning trash or burying it underground? There has to be a better way of managing production, consumption, and how we discard those goods.

Toxic Statistic

In November of 2017, the Times of India published the headline "Air Quality Very Poor - and it's Good News."

An Air Quality Index (AQI) is a number used by governments to communicate the levels of pollution in the air presently and in the future. Many developed nations each have their own version of the AQI system. Thus India's "very poor" AQI rating (considered a good day) in New Delhi is equal to the US AQI rating tagged "Hazardous" and is the highest on the US AQI rating system.[48] "Hazardous" level ratings are described as follows:

- May cause respiratory impact even on healthy people.
- Serious health impacts on people with lung/heart disease.
- The health impacts may be experienced even during light physical activity.

Living in these conditions is an awful reality for hundreds of millions if not billions of people. In 2016, the World Health Organization (WHO) published a worrying statistic. Over 90% of the world's population lives with air pollution over WHO's limits.[49]

The Organization for Economic Co-operation and Development (OECD) published a study in 2016 with additional statistics regarding the power of air pollution:[50]

- Air pollution healthcare costs are projected to rise from 21 billion USD in 2015 to 176 billion USD in 2060.

- The annual number of lost working days in 2060 is projected to reach 3.7 billion (the current count is estimated to be 1.2 billion) at the global level.

- Implementing policies that limit air pollution emissions would lead to improvement in air quality, reduce negative health impacts, and if held accountable can generate substantial benefits for the climate.

Shifting Culture in Education

I think change in action comes from change in culture.

Education is a massive topic, and a great place to begin a culture change is in our colleges and universities. Degree programs for entrepreneurship are certainly a start for supporting a culture of business-builders and problem solvers, but there are more possibilities.

I was recently admitted and launched as a University Innovation Follow (UIF). UIF is a highly-selective program designed to help foster entrepreneurship and innovation among students nationwide. My time with the fellows has taught me so much about the value of innovation, design-thinking, and entrepreneurship for the modern world. At Union College, many improvements to our campus have been initiated, from 3D printing labs to more collaborative work spaces in our campus library. We also help teach courses and workshops on the fundamentals of what we learned from our training.

Why do I bring up this program? If we look at the trend of human development and advancement over time, we grow exponentially in terms of our technological progress and knowledge.[51] At a macro-level, our development looks like a normal exponential curve, but Ray Kurzweil, a renowned intellectual and futurist, goes into more detail with his theories.

Kurzweil explains that progress occurs in "S-curves."[52] Each S-curve is broken down into three phases. The first is slow growth, the early phase of exponential growth. The second is fast growth, the explosive phase that characterizes exponential growth. The third phase is almost like a plateau as the curve levels off.

Why are these S-curves significant? Each curve is a piece of the much larger exponential curve of human development. Each one represents a development, an innovation, or a breakthrough in human ingenuity that pushes us forward as a species. Maximizing the rate at which we discover these (ideally positive) breakthroughs is very important.

Now to bring it back to the story of the UIF program; we have a huge opportunity with programs like the UIF to expand design thinking and entrepreneurship for students of all disciplines. As more students are exposed to this kind of content through workshops and classroom seminars, my hope is that this can help that culture shift.

As the culture changes in our education systems to be more entrepreneurial, it would then be on students to take this knowledge and convert it into action. But what action should we strive for?

Meeting the Intersection

I believe the answer is in something my dearest professor at Union taught me in our social entrepreneurship class:

"The answer lies in the intersection of ideas and industries"

- Professor Harold Fried

Uber is a great example of an intersectional company. Uber jumped on the opportunity to build on the intersection of the poor service taxi industry and the mobile app industry. They're now the dominant ride-sharing service in the United States. Intersections are powerful places to generate value for society.

My aspiration is that through culture change in our educational environments, we can work all the faster towards generational solutions to the problems we have created in our environment.

My hope is to start a movement at the intersection of education culture and entrepreneurship in order to help us solve our problems with the environment faster. The more minds we have working to innovate to generate more S-curves, the greater chance we have at finding those environmental solutions.

While government policies and regulation are certainly good and can have significant impact on the environment, when implemented we cannot rely on them alone to solve this. As the expression goes, "money talks," and big companies that result from innovation have a lot of power too. They can navigate internationally and often have more influence than a government in certain industries or aspects of citizen life.

I support the idea that large businesses are not always evil. They can minimize their cost through economies of scale that would then build better solutions for consumers and governments to use alike. Both of them like cheap goods and services, so why not give it to them and also provide the optimal choice for the environment?

We as a millennial generation need to join and support these culture-changing organizations. This will help us improve the rate at which we can innovate as a society and thus create solutions that allow billions to live in a world where breathing clean air should be the least of their worries.

HAMZA GUMMAN

"Start by doing what's necessary; then do what's possible; and suddenly you are doing the impossible" ~ Francis of Assisi

Who am I?

I am a Brooklyn born United States citizen who has had the pleasure of living in Pakistan for 5 years and experiencing firsthand the countless issues people of third world countries face. I am particularly passionate about educational reform.

What world do I want to live in?

I want to live in a world where the place or socio-economic status you were born in does not define the opportunities you have. In the United States financial aid is often need based, while in Pakistan its test score based. So the well-off that can afford tutors and private schools get scholarships and financial aid, while the vast majority of the poor are denied decent higher education.

How do I see myself as a changemaker?

I see myself as a person who understands first-hand the effect of a proper education on the growth of an individual. People that run these educational institutes are themselves the product of the institution, and people fortunate enough to study abroad have the resources to stay abroad.

If you could choose any changemaker to be your mentor, who would it be ?

I would choose Malala Yousafzai as my mentor, an active advocate for women's education in third world countries and co-founder of Malala Fund. I believe the next step for the Malala fund is to revolutionize the education system that denied women education in the first place.

When They Don't Take You Seriously

Hamza Ghumman

"Brave" and "strong-willed." I could not think of two words that were less characteristic of me, but in naming me Hamza, my parents clearly had aspirations that I was not fulfilling. I was born in the United States and after 5th grade my parents decided to move the family back to Pakistan. At first, I saw it as a positive change: that was just how life is, fast and sometimes abrupt, and I had no choice in the matter but to adapt. However, I began to wonder what kind of future I would have if we stayed in Pakistan. I was able to compete with the high achievers and score in the top percentile, but I felt unfulfilled.

I did not have access to the opportunities and the education I wanted. I was taught that if you work hard, you will be rewarded with opportunity. I saw this was not the case in Pakistan. The basis of student learning was memorization and the emphasis for achievement lay only in test scores. We were not offered extra-curricular activities. There were no internships or clubs besides cricket and soccer. The only focus was academics. I witnessed students routinely cheating and teachers looking the other way. And it reminded me of something Neil deGrasse Tyson had once said: "When students cheat on exams it's because our school system values grades more than students value learning."[53]

I became exhausted during the years I spent in Pakistan and my grades fell along with my interest in school, but I wasn't the only one burning out. I was just one of countless children dissatisfied by the education they were receiving.

Every day it was the same routine: waking up an hour and half before class so we could get ready and beat rush hour traffic. Uniforms were a standard across schools in Pakistan, and they usually consisted of a shirt, tie, dress pants and formal shoes. Since there were at least five big private schools on one small road, traffic could make a 15 minute drive take up to an hour. These schools also had a big student body, as it was normal for a private school to host class grades one to twelve. We stayed in the same class while teachers came to our rooms, so the only time we moved, besides shuffling around, was during lunchtime or physical education. Classes consisted of copying down verbatim what the teacher wrote on the board, and we regurgitated the information during tests and exams. The only way to prepare for exams was to take a couple of weeks to cram the information from our notebooks into our brains, from front to back.

The frustration I felt in this monotonous system was shared by my classmates, but there was no point in airing this anger. When I first said I was going to move back to the U.S., my closest friends simply said: "that is what they all say." I, however, was also the only one I knew in my school with an American passport, and I was fortunate enough to be able to use it again. It took a little over a year of persistently telling my parents we needed to move back for them to finally agree, and the main reason was my education.

One of my closest friends, Talha, ended up going to Western Sydney University in Australia. He barely passed his classes when I knew him in Pakistan. He always said he would pick up in school when he thought it would matter. And he did. When he wanted to apply to Sydney, he started studying more than anyone I knew. He would start studying months ahead for his exams and had the drive to study all day when they came closer. And to my surprise, he scored in the top percentile while most of the high-performing kids I knew burned out by the end.

The both of us, however, had the resources and motivation to move abroad. Talha felt like he could never become the person he wanted to be if he stayed in Pakistan. Now he is finally in an interesting place learning valuable new information every day. I can see his satisfaction for myself in the pictures he sends me once in awhile.

My parents wanted their kids to attend the best private school in the city in Pakistan, even if it strained their budget a bit. Our neighbors, my father's brother, however, thought the local private school was good enough. Since my cousins were much younger than me, I often tutored and tested them. It was during these moments I would see the vast difference in the education we were receiving. Their brightest child, Areeba, who was in the 4th grade, really did know her stuff, but she didn't actually comprehend it.

I remember the first time I tested Areeba. I wrote down verbatim questions from her notebook, yet she couldn't answer some of them even though she had answered them perfectly before. I was surprised. Then her mother informed me that the only reason Areeba failed to answer some of the questions was because I changed the order. Yes, Areeba also memorized the order of the answers, but in changing the order she couldn't tell which answer went to which question. I was shocked when her mother told me it really is just the same questions in the same order on all of her tests. Once, during a math tutoring session, when even my tutor didn't understand how my teacher had derived the answer, he told me I didn't need to waste so much time trying to understand it. I could just simply memorize the steps. I was once again shocked.

While this issue in comprehension is somewhat mitigated at higher levels when students start to grasp English, memorization still remains the key to high grades. I was curious to put this experience into context, so I read a *New York Times* article titled "What's Really Keeping Pakistan's Children Out of School?" This piece explained that, "A vast number of aspirational families in Pakistan invest a large proportion of their income in educating their children at low-cost private schools. They do not speak English at home but they demand English at school, because it is the language of the elite and the global marketplace. So Pakistan's private schools use English textbooks and tests, even though 94% of private-school teachers don't know English. A result is that the children are rote learning to get through tests in a language they don't understand. By the time these students get to a university, where the medium of instruction is English, they are copying their papers from the internet without consequence. Plagiarism is not just a norm; it is a necessity."[54]

Speaking of necessity...there are many colleges in the American school systems that offer extensive need-based aid. What I found unsettling in Pakistan was that it was often the students that went to elite schools with private tutors that were the ones awarded score-based scholarships. Poverty kept many students from a decent education. As such, "faced with a choice between having a child help in the fields or learn nothing at school, many parents rationally pick the former."

The difference in enrollment between children of the richest and poorest fifth of households is greater in Pakistan than in all but two of the 96 developing countries recently analyzed by the World Bank."[55] The reason child labor is an unresolved issue in Pakistan is because of the failing education system. Parents living in poverty often think that it would be more beneficial to ensure their child knows a profession by placing them in a workplace from an early age, than to send them to a public school with no job opportunities afterwards. It is the hope of scoring in the top percentile, studying constantly for months, that motivates many poor students. However in the end, sadly, "Most Pakistani children who start school drop out by the age of nine; just 3% of those starting public school graduate from 12th grade, the final year."[56]

I hope to encourage at least a discussion among students on how they could start to take initiative on making their own schools a healthier learning environment. I know it is not always possible for kids to take control of their own education like I did. That's why it is all the more important to make the system they *are* in as enriching as possible through initiatives like after-school programs, such as a robotics club or a philosophy club.

The first step could be to gather enough people interested in starting an unofficial club, and later approaching the faculty for support. In the worst case scenario, the club proposal is rejected, but that should not stop the students from continuing to meet and work on what they enjoy. With enough extracurriculars, school would start to become a place where students can grow outside the classroom and apply what they learned. Once students realize the information they have been memorizing in class can have more applications than regurgitation on exams and tests, the educational system can start to shift. It will be a very slow process, but students will finally have a reason to go into classes less worried about memorization and more interested in understanding what is being taught. Critical thinking will finally overtake regurgitation of knowledge.

The power I found inside myself when my parents agreed to move back to the US has given me an entirely new perspective on life. I have an obligation to show my parents that we made the right decision and I owe it to myself to take advantage of the opportunities available in the United States. I now see that I have the ability to determine my own future. I have become brave and strong-willed when it comes to defining my life path. I have used these qualities to not only excel academically, but to throw myself into the life of my school and my new home. Education in Pakistan showed me the value of learning in a school community that happens outside of the classroom. While I will always value my academics, I have found that the experiences through which I am able to apply what I have learned force me to grow and learn the most.

PHOEBE HALLAHAN

"Don't take life seriously, because you won't come out of it alive."
~Warren Miller

Who am I?

I was born in 1997 and grew up in Arlington, MA. I am a Film and Environmental Science Major with an Art history minor. Traveling the world and taking pictures while trying new foods, meeting different people, and experiencing unfamiliar cultures would hit on many of my interests. Fun fact: I am a top nationally ranked freestyle skier and have competed with/against olympians on many occasions.

What world do I want to live in?

I want to live in a world with peace, minimal suffering, and equality for all in all situations. I sound like a pageant queen with this response but in a utopian world of my creating, this is what it would be.

What is a characteristic that you would like to change in yourself?

I wish I had more natural drive. I will get projects done well and on time, but I often feel like I have to try hard to motivate myself, even to do things I love. If a person has no talent but great drive I believe that they can get further than a person with natural talent but no drive. You have to have grit!

If you could choose any changemaker to be your mentor, who would it be?

Pamela Castro is one of my favorite millennial activists. She is based out of Brazil and uses graffiti, a male dominated art form, to raise awareness about violence against women. She has also started a program called "Rede Nami" that runs workshops for all ages to educate communities on domestic violence.

My Television Romance

Phoebe Hallahan

My family leads a spontaneous lifestyle. It's more fun to randomly pick a hotel when we get there than to book it weeks in advance, like most other families do. But maybe the word I should be using is "uncertainty." "Spontaneous," to me, involves fun while "uncertainty" is comprised of stress. It is stressful to be driving around at 9 pm in an unfamiliar state trying to figure out if any hotels have a vacancy.

My childhood always had a sense of uncertainty to it. We moved a lot and my dad seemed to be laid off every year, sometimes less, no matter how many sleepless nights he spent on work. On course this spilled into the rest of my life, my first year of high school seemed to be filled with uncertainty too. Would I get drunk like my friends on Friday? Would I still have friends when I didn't want to drink? Would the junior boys become obsessed with me as they had with my best friends?

The only constant in my life was at 7:30 am every weekday: *Arthur*. Yes, that *Arthur*. The animated children's TV show on PBS Kids about an aardvark and his adventures in the third grade. I was late to homeroom countless times so that I could watch the entire episode. There was something calming and routine knowing that every morning, no matter what uncertainty had happened the day before, at 7:30, Arthur would come "walking down the street" on my T.V. screen.

The summer after my freshman year of high school, in a moment of spontaneity (or uncertainty) my family decided to moved from Boston, where I had lived my whole life, to Park City, Utah. We arrived two weeks before school began. I didn't know anyone, we didn't have a house, and my parents didn't have jobs. Those circumstances, in and of themselves, were a set up for a tough year. After the first few months, falling in love was the last thing I expected to happen.

But it happened. It has been six years since then, and I will never forget Joey climbing through Dawson's window. Yes, the love I am referring to is not between myself and another human being, but between myself and a high school drama series that aired on T.V. on Tuesdays, fifteen years prior.

If you have never watched Dawson's Creek...READ THIS![57]

> *Dawson's Creek "was both a sweet nod to coming-of-age stories and a bold and sometimes controversial addition to the teen genre. Budding filmmaker Dawson, goofy troublemaker Pacey, moody tomboy Joey, and reformed-ish bad girl Jen all discover the joy and (mostly) pain of first love as they date and break up and date and break up... and date and break up, all with the titular body of water as a soothing backdrop. Love triangles and rectangles are nothing new, but Creek's delivery of these topics was shockingly fresh. These pubescent pals weren't going to the Peach Pit for shakes — they were talking about masturbating to Katie Couric and having affairs with their teachers. And they spoke about their hormonal escapades (or lack thereof) in smart, Aaron Sorkin-esque dialogue."*

For those of you who have not been to Park City, it is a town lodged between mountain peaks and home to the world famous Sundance film festival, but it attracts celebrities year round. The town is known for its skiing. There are three big mountains all within seven minutes of each other including the renowned upscale Deer Valley Ski Resort, host to the 2002 Olympics. Justin Bieber, Michael Jordan, and Lisa Kudrow are among the list of celebrities who have houses there. The mothers fulfill the stereotype of "trophy-wife" and their children would never be caught in sweatpants.

That being said, Park City has some of the friendliest humans I have met. They loved spending their weekends in the mountains, camping in the summers and skiing in the winters. Writing this now, Park City almost seems like paradise. Except that my family was far from wealthy and I loved my sweatpants.

Driving to school, the sun would be just rising and perfectly blinding. Lunch was eaten in the back hallway. Sometimes in the halls people would smile or wave in my direction, and I would have to catch myself before waving back when I would realize that the wave was meant for someone behind me. One day, I thought I saw this girl I knew from elementary school. Back then I had despised her, but for those few moments my heart raced and I almost smiled and ran up to her. I was so happy to see a familiar face. Of course, it was not her and my heart sank and a lump in my throat appeared that would have made my voice choke if someone had actually spoken to me.

We lived in hotels for the first few weeks when we arrived since we had not bought a home prior to moving. Eventually we moved into a three-room apartment over somebody else's garage, adjacent to their mansion. My younger brother and I not only shared a bedroom, but a bed.

There was no space to be alone, so I would go out for hours on end just to be able to breathe. I would come home with bright red cheeks and hands numb and swollen from the cold. I would often call my friend from home but some days I couldn't even speak without my voice cracking as the tears trickled down my cheeks. I didn't want to be crying, but I couldn't help it. I wanted to feel my friend, feel the warmth of her body as we hugged. Instead, all I had was the empty air of our voices through the phone two thousand miles away from each other.

No, this is not a story of my battle with depression or anything deeper than the fundamental feelings of sadness, loneliness, and the pain that comes with physical aching for something unattainable.

The night before school began I found myself in a ball on the cold porcelain of the bathtub. The warm water rushing from the shower head was just loud enough to muffle my crying, nay my wailing. The water cleared my cheeks of tears in time for new ones to fall and my naked body to shudder. I felt so far away from everything I knew. I felt so alone, and I believe, for the first and honestly only time in my life (thus far), I felt completely hopeless.

I mean, I am here, writing this story for you now so not all hope was lost as I survived that year. Truth be told, by the end of my time there, I had made friends that would make me sad to leave. How did I get through it you might ask? Well, the aforementioned love that I found was what kept me gasping for air when I could have drowned.

I had begun watching a sitcom, "Don't Trust the B in Apartment 23," before moving to Utah. The show was canceled after less than a year. However, James Van Der Beek a.k.a Dawson from *Dawson's Creek*, starred in it as himself. The show would reference *Dawson's Creek*, and with high accolades, so I decided to check it out.

Thank goodness for the rise of Netflix around this time as it had the entire series. Dawson's was at my fingertips whenever I wanted or needed it. I believe I became so invested because they were the "friends" I hung out with after school. I would come home and watch an episode or two (...or more) of Dawson's to pass the time until bed. It was easier to go home and enter a television universe than stay in my own lonely one.

I began to disassociate with my own life, which was at that time, for lack of a better word, sad, and I began to absorb *Dawson's Creek*. I watched Joey in her loneliness and felt less alone. I watched Jen erase her past and start anew, which made me feel hopeful. I watched Dawson dream and have his heartbroken repeatedly, and I knew that it was all going to be alright. As each character went through their own hardships, I was able to forget about mine.

It happened quickly, the attachment. I think Joey was the first character that resonated with me. She was a stubborn tomboy who preferred her guy friends to girls. Still, one of the more affecting episodes, although they were all jam-packed with drama, was the season 1 finale.[58] Joey and Dawson visit her scum father, who cheated on her dying mother in prison. She and her father have an emotional exchange as they lock fingers through the metal fence and we see Joey cry for one of the first times. Watching such a strong character give in and breakdown was powerful. In a manner, it made me feel like it was okay to cry. Obviously my circumstances were quite different than those of Joey Potters but, nonetheless, she made me okay with not being okay.

There were episodes of Dawson's during which I cried while watching, but in reality I was crying for myself and my own life; the show was just an excuse. I think that everybody deserves an outlet. For me it was TV. I honestly attribute surviving my year in Utah, along with assimilation back in Boston, to Dawson and his friends. And for that, they will always hold a place in my heart.

Video ~~Killed the Radio Star~~ Saved Everything

My generation is notoriously associated with being attached to our devices. We walk with our heads down, glued to our screens that fit in the palm of our hands. Older people tend to critique how much TV we watch or why kids are always playing video games, but sometimes these things are escapes more than entertainment. Through video games, introverts (along with everyone else) are able to play, connect, and communicate with others online. Video games open a new world, one in which they are able to connect to people they would otherwise have no contact with. Some people build strong friendships with their online companions. These fantasy worlds are the same as the ones found on TV shows. Both video games and television have strong fanbases for specific games or shows. People are able to come together at events such as Comic-Con where they can fully emerge themselves in the world or culture of the TV show or game. These events have huge turnouts, people come dressed in costume…lots of John Snows. A mutual fascination and enjoyment creates an entire universe dedicated to the realities that entertainment has built. False realities allow people to escape their own and focus on other people's battles or drama. Our absorption into another life, whether it be real or computer animated, allows for an outlet.

Recently there has been a spike in gay and bisexual characters, especially main ones on TV. This shift in casting and character developments has made some spectators uncomfortable. However, this is huge for the currently underrepresented LGBTQ+ community. Lizzie Plaugic explains that, "As the number of LGBTQ characters on television increases, more people around the world will have the opportunity to see themselves represented on-screen — sometimes for the first time ever."[59] Straight cisgender people see themselves constantly in television shows or movies and have no shortage of role models. We, as a society, are slowly

Generation Now: Millennials Call for Social Change

It is with deep admiration that I give thanks to you,
this awe-inspiring group of changemakers.
You prove that humanity and kindness
—wrapped in fearless courage—
can change our lives, one word and one person at a time.
I thank you!

~ Christine Henseler

Made in United States
North Haven, CT
03 January 2024

moving in the right direction by having more LGBTQ+ characters. These characters will greatly impact future generations.

Shay Mitchell, who plays a lesbian on Freeform's *Pretty Little Liars* has spoken many times about the letters and DMs she has received. LGBTQ+ youth reach out to her and thank her for character, Emily Fields, who has given them the courage to finally come out to their family and friends or embrace their sexuality.[60] It is small gestures such as this that show how important and impactful representation in TV and in movies can be.

Pop culture has led to a world where people see themselves in the characters on screens. Young girls have gained many a role model in the past decade, notably Katniss Everdeen of *The Hunger Games*. Strong female leads are proving to children that women can be successful, strong, powerful people whether they are businesswomen, dancers, scientists, or even the villain. When was the last time that you saw a female play a badass bad guy?

2017 saw the release of *Wonder Woman*, the first feature superhero movie about a female superhero. 2017! You know how many male superhero movies were produced before then? Over 50. I saw *Wonder Woman* three times in theaters and left awestruck each time. Gal Gadot's portrayal was spectacular, I wish I had had a Wonder Woman to aspire me when I was a kid.

This year (2018) *Black Panther* became the first feature superhero movie to headline a predominantly black cast. Frederick Joseph, a New Yorker who started a GoFundMe campaign for a Boys & Girls club to see *Black Panther*, stated that it is a "rare opportunity for young students (primarily of color) to see a black major cinematic and comic book character come to life. This representation is truly fundamental for young people, especially those who are often underserved, unprivileged, and marginalized both nationally and globally".⁶¹ Nathan D. B. Connolly, a historian, said that *Black Panther* was "a breakthrough in black cultural representation."⁶² The movie was well-received, breaking grossing records in its opening weekend.⁶³ This diversity is important and should be a continuing trend in entertainment.

The screen, in all its forms - Netflix, Youtube, Playstation etc. - is a staple for the Millennials and Gen Z'ers. Nicknamed the virtual generation and iGen, Generation Z and the ones that follow will progressively become more dependent on what is projected on our screens. Technology will be so integrated into the coming generations that they will not know a world without screens.

Television changed my life, as I assume it has done for millions of others. It is not deserving of the negative label it has received. I am not saying that everyone hates TV or video games or music videos, but it should be acknowledged that TV does not always have a good representation. Television and all that is launched onto the screens in our world have the power to be just as positive and life-altering.

The future of the entertainment industry is in our hands. We must write the future with strong female leads, no whitewashing, less stereotyping, and raw, realistic material. These influences have the power to change people's lives and make the world a better place. TV and movies tell stories, they convey the trials, adventures, romance, and the emotion that comes with life. I am thankful for television's positive impacts on my life, and I wish to see more acknowledgement for the power of television and how screens might just be saving our generation's lives.

BROOKE MACKENZIE

"There is nothing noble in being superior to your fellow man; true nobility is being superior to your former self."

~ *Ernest Hemingway*

Who am I?

I am a Psychology major and Political Science minor at Union College (NY) class of 2018. I am the oldest of 7 siblings and an avid animal lover. In my free time I am likely practicing yoga or enjoying the company of those I love.

How do I see myself as a changemaker?

Goals can be terminal, but when they are driven by a passion they become a cause you are dedicated to seeing a change in. Studying mental health was my goal in college and now ending the stigma has become my passion.

Having grown up in our current world, society has taught me that mental health needs to be addressed head on. I have lost fellow classmates to self-harm, lost teachers to domestic violence, and had those close to me struggle to cope with different aspects of their life. For me, situations like these could have been prevented with the right education, support, and empathy.

What world do I want to live in?

I want to live in a world where there is integration across all health services and we address the mind and body as a whole. This is a world where people are educated and taught positive habits in managing their mental health from a young age, and where the stigma against receiving counseling services is broken. This is a world I am prepared and dedicated to help create.

Who is someone who has inspired you?

My previous supervisor and now dear friend, Benjamin Weiner, is someone who has mentored and inspired me to stand up for myself and for others as we are not always capable of doing that ourselves.

Can You Hear Me or Am I Crazy?

Brooke Mackenzie

Looking back always seems to be easy, perhaps that's why people say hindsight is 20/20. Looking back on my childhood I see so many different versions of myself. However, the one thing that remains consistent is that I never felt I had a voice. When I was sad I was offered an object to cheer me up, when I was grumpy I was told to walk it off, and when I was happy I was told to settle down. It seemed that every emotion I expressed was somehow wrong. Moving through grade school I saw my peers reprimanded or excused from class because they were "causing a scene," when in fact they were really just expressing themselves. Reminiscing on these memories paints a darker picture of what was really a form of institutionalized emotional oppression. What may seem like a dramatic stretch of events is actually something that has created deep rooted, negative effects in our society.

When I sat down to write my personal statement for graduate school, I was faced with the ever existential question of "why?" Why did I care about mental health? Why did I spend four years studying it? And why am I bothering to pursue a career in it? For me these questions led to an evaluation of what I wanted to get out of life. What would get me to the end of the road and allow me to look back with a sense of completion?

The answer gradually became more clear. I care because no one did when I was growing up. No one cared that my classmates or I did not know how to manage the growing ball of emotions inside us. No one thought to teach us the warning signs for eating disorders, depression, or abuse. All anyone cared about was making sure students were walking in single file lines, increasing standardized testing scores, and criticizing girls for their spaghetti straps. And at the end of the day, I want to be able to know people have been given the tools they need to lead happier and healthier lives; the tools my classmates and I lacked.

Looking back on my childhood I began to wonder: if my classmates and I had been given these platforms to express ourselves, would things have been different? If we had been taught how to identify emotions within ourselves and in others, would our lives be on different trajectories? Perhaps open discussions, seminars, or electives on topics such as hormonal and emotional development, mental health and illness, or how to create discussion could have better prepared us for what we were dealing with and what was to come. If we had been taught to recognize the warning signs of domestic violence, would our English teacher still be here today? If we had been shown the signs of self harm, would some of our classmates be here to walk with us at graduation? Would I have recognized the signs of depression and been able to support my best friend sooner so he knew he was not alone? Could I have avoided the nightmares I get every night?

There are too many scenarios to rework, but the bottom line is that while some things cannot be prevented, they could have been managed. Management comes in so many different forms: for some this could be getting treatment or education and for others this could be getting the support they needed from their friends and family. There is no perfect formula for mental health, nor is there any particular way a person is supposed to feel. Each person's emotions are their own to enjoy and express. The worst crime we could commit in a society, as connected as we are today, is to make someone feel alone or unworthy. As members of society, we need to start seeing each other and recognizing that we live in a vastly diverse world filled with beautiful people with varying degrees of mental health.

What Are Our Competitors Doing That We Aren't?

The U.S. seems to have fallen short in the education of its youth on mental health whereas other countries have decided to face this task head on. The World Health Organization (WHO) has partnered with a group of European countries to form the Joint Action on Mental Health and Wellbeing initiative. This organization formed as a result of compelling data showing that, "10-20% of children and adolescents worldwide experience mental disorders, which if untreated, severely influence their development, educational attainment and their potential to live fulfilling lives."[64]

This data is not exclusive to European countries, so why is it that these are the only countries currently addressing said issue? The solution is not to simply teach a class or apologize and say we will do better next time. Mental health is a comprehensive topic that touches all aspects of life, including impacting the economic health of a country. As the prevalence rates continue to rise, so do the estimated economic costs. Currently the costs are averaging between seven to sixty-four thousand Euros per child as a consequence of mental health issues being ignored and the proper care being neglected.[65] On top of these extraordinary costs, "mental illness has increasingly been recognized as the most significant health concern for children and adolescents in developed countries."[66]

Children need help, they need to be taught, and they need to be heard. It is not uncommon to wind up finding all roads leading to childhood development when searching for the root of an issue. Scientists say we undergo crucial developmental changes all the way into our early twenties. On top of this, research has shown that "up to 50% of lifetime mental disorders arise before adulthood."[67] Despite the data, and despite all the mantras, and the warnings, somehow children still end up ignored, silenced, or discredited for being at the tail end of the social hierarchy. Yet, once we enter into adulthood and gain our footing, the damage is already done and it is often irreversible.

The World Health Organization has recognized the ubiquity of mental health and how it culminates over time. Moving forward, the Joint Action on Mental Health and Wellbeing initiative is not just integrating programs into the education systems, but also in the workplaces and in community centers. This is what we should strive for: total integration of mental health in society. This comes from recognizing its role in everyday life and respecting the fact that everyone comes from a different background with different needs.

Personal Initiative

The biggest change we can make is with our voice. I challenge you to break the silence and speak out about these issues, both on an institutional scale and from the heart. The more we make this a normal part of daily conversation, the more we reduce the stigma until eventually we live in a world of acceptance.

To get involved on a larger scale, check out Mental Health in America (MHA) or National Alliance on Mental Illness (NAMI). MHA advocates for a preventative approach and NAMI is a non profit organization with an impressive presence across the U.S. Sign up for emails from both organizations for chances to donate or volunteer!

To bring mental health awareness to your school check out Active Minds at activeminds.org or see if your school already has a chapter!

DIY

What is a small-scale change that you can make starting today to promote your mission?

ANNA MAHONY

"Twenty years from now you will be more disappointed by the things you didn't do than by the things you did."

~ Mark Twain

Who am I?

I was born in 1998 in Schenectady, NY, and I've lived in this area my whole life! I'm a chemistry major and psychology minor who is very passionate about the environment. I also love the Adirondacks, theater, and food.

What does changemaker mean to you?

A changemaker is someone who sees a problem in the world and takes it upon themselves to help find a solution to that issue. They don't just sit back and let the word continue the way it is. The change they induce does not have to be monumentally large; even if they fix one small problem in the world, its progress.

What world do I want to live in?

I want to live in a world where people care about both their neighbors and the environment around them. Ideally, a world in which all people are treated equally and no one is hateful. It sounds really cheesy, but I want to live in a world of acceptance and love. While I know this is idealistic and likely impossible, by showing kindness to others each day, I believe we can come a little bit closer to that goal everyday.

Why is social change such an important issue, especially today?

To me, social change is important, especially to our generation, because we have tools readily available to us that were not there before. Because of the internet and social media, we are more connected than ever before and it is much easier to communicate information with others. There are a lot of problems in this world that have existed for many years and it is time to do something about it. I believe we can really accomplish change if we try.

Life in Plastic is Not Fantastic

Anna Mahony

The biggest cliché I've heard at college has been: "studying abroad totally changed my life." Without fail, everyone I know who has studied abroad has told me some version of this - that it was amazing or that it changed their outlook on the world. Each time I heard it, I'd politely nod my head and listen to their stories while thinking to myself that it was just one of those things everyone says.

But then it happened to me. Not on a big scale; after all, I was only abroad for three weeks, but it did change the way I thought about one thing in particular.

This past winter I got the chance to study abroad in New Zealand, a country with an overflowing amount of natural beauty. *Everywhere* I went, *everything* was gorgeous. I don't think I've ever appreciated nature more. There were rainforests with trees so tall you could barely see the tops and lakes so pristinely blue they seemed fake. I hiked glaciers and volcanoes and even a mountain right next to Mount Doom from *Lord of the Rings*. I stargazed on a beach in the middle of nowhere at 3 a.m. during the biggest meteor shower of the year. Words don't do it justice (another very cliché thing to say, but it's true). I never wanted to leave, and as I write this, I want to go back.

One day, we made a quick stop at an overlook in a national park. It was breathtaking. Everything was so lush and so green, and you could see for miles in every direction. Off to the side, there was a sign about the park that I walked over to read. As I scanned it, I learned that national parks cover 10% of New Zealand's total land area. I thought to myself something I'd thought several times throughout my trip: that it was amazing how much this country cared about protecting the environment. Ironically, later that day, I learned that President Trump announced a plan to slash the size of two national parks here in the United States to allow for more oil and gas drilling. The stark contrast between New Zealand and the U.S. stood out to me right then. We are backtracking instead of making strides forward.

Many countries, New Zealand included, are making environmental issues a priority, and as a country, we are doing the opposite. If we continue down this path, we are headed toward disaster. Before this trip, I'd already been passionate about sustainability and the environment, but something about this experience turned that spark of interest into something much bigger. It was there in New Zealand that I recognized I needed to do more to help create positive change at home.

How I Became Passionate about the Environment

While at my friend Emily's house one day this winter, I asked where the recycling bin was so I could recycle my plastic soda bottle. "We don't have one," she responded. "Just throw it in the trash." I was astonished. It hadn't occurred to me that not everyone has recycling bins. I was so surprised that I asked "Why not?" and simply received an apathetic shrug and an off-handed "Oh, I don't know" in return.

I had a similar experience while shopping for college with my soon-to-be roommate, Kim. I decided to buy a second trash can to use as a recycling bin in our room. She asked why I had bought two. And when I excitedly explained my idea to her, she laughed and said, "Oh Anna..." while shaking her head, as if the idea were silly. When we moved in, there was a giant recycling bin right outside our door, but I still kept the one I bought. It always surprises me when I come into the room and see her throwing papers or plastic bottles in the trash instead of the recycling bin in our room or in the big one, which is two feet away from our room in the hallway.

I don't think these reactions are uncommon. It's so easy to forget about the waste we create. We throw things in the trash and they disappear into a garbage truck a few days later, never to be seen by us again. We don't see the huge landfills our waste goes to, or the tons of plastic floating in the ocean that is harmful to wildlife. It's easy not to care about environmental issues unless you are directly affected by their negative impacts.

One of the main reasons I began to care about the environment is because I come from a household that tries to be environmentally friendly. We save bags to use again and make sure to separate recyclables from garbage. Growing up, my family also talked about environmental issues with me.

I was eight when my mom took me to see the new movie *Happy Feet*, which was about a cute little penguin who tap dances. I was super excited, and as a third grader, I was still really into cartoons. It was the kind of movie I usually loved, and I'm sure I did enjoy it a lot at the time. However, twelve years later the only scene I remember is the one in which a funky looking penguin named Lovelace gets a plastic six-pack ring stuck around his neck.[68] The poor little guy couldn't get it off and none of the other penguins could help him. They just had to watch as he struggled to breathe. Watching this scene stressed me out, and I remember spending the rest of the movie hoping that that didn't happen to penguins in real life.

Afterwards, I was still worried about the penguins, so, knowing she would have the answer, I asked my mom about it. And, of course, she did have the answer. But it wasn't the answer I wanted to hear. She told me that this did happen to penguins, and other animals as well, which is why she always made sure to cut up plastic rings before throwing them out. The small pieces of plastic can still be a problem, but cutting them up is better than nothing. Since then, whenever I'm about to throw out plastic rings, I'm always reminded of that scene in *Happy Feet*, and I make sure to cut them up.

Two years later, I went through what I can only call a "recycling phase." Yeah, I'll admit it - that's pretty weird for a 5th grader. A lot of kids go through an emo phase or a boyband phase; I went through a recycling phase. I became hyper-aware of which products were recyclable or not, absolutely despised styrofoam, and began using recycled items for many of my DIY projects. My sister and I used to do tons of arts and crafts, and I still have some of the containers we made from Kleenex boxes to hold toys and nail polish and such. None of this was particularly impactful. I wasn't some "10-year old saving the world." In fact, I still remember the feeling of shock when I first heard that most of what we "recycle" does not get recycled at all.[69]

It seems ironic to me that even while I was trying to do little things to help the earth, in reality I wasn't doing much. I had thought I was making a bigger difference, and it wasn't until later that I realized the most important part of "reduce, reuse, and recycle" was, in fact, reducing. Had there been a bigger focus on environmental literacy in my education, I might have learned this earlier.

The Importance of Environmental Education

If there was a greater emphasis on environmental concerns early on in our education in the United States, perhaps more would be done to combat climate change. Project Green Schools did a study in the U.S. investigating environmental education in public schools. For over 50% of the schools, the environmental club was the primary way to learn about the environment.[70] This led to the conclusion that environmental education is not integrated into typical classes.⁷¹ Overall, this study showed that public schools are having trouble making this a priority, but in this day and age, it needs to be a primary issue.

Another study was conducted in the form of an exam to test Michigan State University students' environmental knowledge compared to American adults without a college education. The results showed that about a quarter of the college students knew a lot about the environment and got high scores on the test; however, the average grade was a C, meaning the majority of scores were low.⁷² Adult Americans without college education scored much lower. The authors of this study concluded that there should be more education at the K-12 level in order to increase the amount of environmental knowledge of high school graduates.⁷³

The good news is that there are organizations working to improve this knowledge gap in the United States. For instance, the North American Association for Environmental Education (NAAEE) has been working to increase environmental literacy across all states by integrating it into K-12 education.⁷⁴ This initiative is doing a lot of good work but has faced many obstacles due to lack of time and resources as well as cuts to education funding in public schools.⁷⁵

Here at Union College, I'm very involved in the Chemistry & Biochemistry Club. Another club officer and I have been working on initiatives to teach kids about chemistry. Recently, we went to an after-school program called Girls Inc. in Schenectady where we worked with a group of about 12 girls ranging in ages from 8-11. When we asked if they had heard of global climate change most of them half-heartedly raised their hands. We then followed up and asked what they knew about it, but no one could answer. In fact, not all of them were super into the activity that followed. But, there were a handful of girls who seemed interested and wrote down notes to themselves to make sure they remembered what we told them. One little girl excitedly told us that she was going to teach her mom all about greenhouse gases when she got home.

The experience overall was both good and bad. It made us a little sad to realize these girls hadn't had much education about climate change. But, Marie thought the event went well because *even if only one girl had learned something from us, it was a success*. More education regarding our environment would not necessarily impact everyone, but even if it makes a few people think about the environment more and make small lifestyle changes, it would be an improvement.

As Individuals, What Can We Do?

Unfortunately, the current administration in the United States is not putting an emphasis on environmental issues. If anything, they've doing the opposite. In the past, we have put rules and regulations in place to attempt to solve problems relating to climate change. However, this has recently changed.

In April 2018, the U.S. administration proposed rollbacks on the United States' biggest effort to minimize carbon emissions. In March, the Federal Emergency Management Agency (FEMA) expelled the word "climate change" from its strategic plan, despite the numbers of intense storms that have impacted the nation throughout this year. The government also proposed numerous cuts to programs dedicated to environmental research and renewable energy, such as eliminating the EPA's climate-change research program from the annual budget.[76] The EPA has also loosened regulations on toxic air pollution by dropping the "once in, always in" policy which aimed to "lock in reductions of hazardous air pollution." These are just a few of the many cuts, rollbacks, and other regulations put in place that will ultimately harm the environment.[77] These are very serious, negative changes. If the EPA does not put an emphasis on environmental consciousness and research, it becomes increasingly more difficult for positive change to occur.

While the current situation is rather depressing and discouraging, there are many countries that are doing great things for the environment. New Zealand plans to have 90% of its electricity generated by renewable sources by 2025, and that number was already at 79% as of 2011.[78] The Netherlands recently introduced the world's first plastic-free grocery aisle, with more than 700 plastic-free products available.[79] Rwanda, and many other countries, have completely outlawed plastic bags, and Indonesia is planning to be plastic bag-free by 2021.[80] These countries and more are all making strides toward a better future for our planet.

The reason Indonesia will be plastic bag-free by 2021 is because of two young changemakers, Melati and Isabel Wisjen, who saw a problem in their community and decided to do something about it.[81] These girls started the foundation "Bye Bye Plastic Bags" (BBBP) and because of their hard work and determination, they've been able to create positive environmental change in their country.[82] Indonesia contributes 10% of the world's plastic waste and the efforts of these two young girls will help change that. It started as the simple goal of an 8-year-old and a 10-year-old and now there are 17 teams worldwide. Now teenagers, these girls organized a beach clean-up that more than 12,000 people attended.

There is a common belief that one or two people cannot make a difference, so it is not worth trying. In order for change to begin, a person needs to have determination and confidence in their ability to create change. So often when I'm in a rush, it's easy to think it's not worth going the extra mile (or extra inch, to be honest) to find a recycling bin instead of a trash can. It's easy to think that just one item won't have a negative impact when so many are used or thrown away each day. But if that's everyone's mindset, then nothing will ever change.

500 million plastic straws are thrown away every day in the United States. That adds up to about 1.6 straws per person, and between the ages of 5 and 65, the average person will use 38,000 straws.[83] The EPA has stated that over 380 billion plastic bags are used every year and about 6 million plastic cups are thrown away every day in America.[84] A total of 260 million tons of plastic is produced each year, 10% of which will end up in the ocean.[85] This frightening amount of plastic has harmful effects on the quality of the water, as well as aquatic life and other animals. When plastic ends up in the sea, it takes hundreds of years to degrade and, eventually, breaks down into toxic particles.[86] It is incredibly sad that our carelessness is causing animals to suffer and die at alarming rates. Plastic is everywhere nowadays, but life in plastic really is not fantastic. If we stopped using many one-use plastic products it could really make a positive difference.

One person can make change. It might happen slowly, and the impact might not be immediately visible, but working towards a healthier planet is an important goal. If one person decided not to use straws anymore, there would be 38,000 less thrown out in their lifetime, all because of that one person. What is the point of using a plastic product when you'll just throw it away after one use, but it'll stick around for hundreds of years? Personally, I'm trying to stop using plastic straws even when it's an easy option, and I've completely stopped buying bottled water even if I forget my reusable bottle at home. I'm also trying not to take plastic bags at stores anymore. Since my "recycling phase," I've always been passionate about the environment, but now I'm actively working to reduce my use of plastics as well.

With a combination of increasing environmental literacy through environmental education and making small changes to our lifestyles, we as Millennials can create change. There are many ways we can help the environment. We can do this by supporting organizations like the North American Association for Environmental Education and by reducing the use of plastics in our everyday lives, to name a few. Small changes add up to make big differences. Even if we can't see them, the change is occurring. It might save one little penguin's life or make our planet a little greener. And if that happens, I think it will be worth it. It's time to stop taking steps back and start making strides toward a better future for our Earth. She deserves it.

DISCLAIMER: All names have been changed in this article for the privacy of the people involved.

KATE OSTERHOLZ

"Beliefs are choices. First you choose your beliefs. Then your beliefs affect your choices." ~ Roy T. Bennett

Who am I?

Kate Osterholtz, b.1998. I grew up in a small town in Southern New Hampshire in a Quaker household. I am currently in my first year at Union College and am studying anthropology and am on the pre-Law track. I am passionate about dogs, empowering women and making mistakes

Why is social change such an important issue, especially today having so much information available all the time?

I think social change is one of the most important issues presented to our generation. We are the generation of status-quo breakers and norm-shifters and that is a powerful tool. It is easy to get bogged down with all the information constantly thrown at us. It seems like there are so many issues to back and bandwagons to hop on; it can be overwhelming. But finding one movement that lights a fire under you, then diving in is unbelievably powerful. With all the information out there today, each and every one of us can explore the changemaker within us, big or small.

What world do I want to live In?

I know that I do not want to live in a perfect world. I think there is something to be found within the flaws. I would like a world that has conflict, but also resolution, one that has peace but still strives for the better. I want to live in a world that embraces challenge and allows for everyone to live the life they deserve.

What does the term changemaker mean to me?

I think the terms "Millennial" and "changemaker" now go hand in hand. Growing up, I always thought of a changemaker as someone like Martin Luther King Jr., Ghandi or Malala Yousafzai. I thought change could only be created by those who have beat unbelievable odds. I now know that there is a changemaker within all of us. Changemakers don't have to be life-altering or earth-shattering; they appear in all different forms. Simply showing up and making noise and shouting-out for the issues that empower you, that's what makes a changemaker.

The Birds and Bees and Everything In Between

Kate Osterholtz

I still remember it three years later. I don't think about it often and usually only for a moment, but I do remember it. To be honest, that surprises me. It wasn't life-altering or earth-shattering, and I don't think I felt any different the next day, but nonetheless I remember it. It was all very nonchalant and frankly quite unfulfilling. Yet, it mattered. It mattered SO much. It mattered to the girl three seats down in math class and to the sophomore boy on the soccer team. It mattered to my best friend, Lindsey, and to my mom, and it maybe even mattered to him, but it didn't really matter to me.

It was just sex. It wasn't special or magical or anything like they talk about, but it happened, and for me that was it. But looking back now, it did matter. But I didn't allow myself to let it matter. I was ready to have sex. I did it, and that was all. I refused to dwell on it or allow it to be a topic of conversation, and I think that's really disappointing. I was too afraid of critique or shame that I thought if I didn't care then nobody else would. But because of this mindset, I did not allow myself to process this truly formative experience.

If I were to go back three years and talk to my younger self, the first thing I would say is "you go girl." I would throw myself a goddamn party and celebrate my decision. Then I would say that it wasn't special or magical, and that that is ok. It happened, I chose for it to happen and that is all that mattered. I don't think that was said enough. I, as a young woman, have learned in my (albeit limited) experience that sometimes it matters, and sometimes it doesn't. And that's okay. That's part of sex and sex is part of life. I would high-five her for being safe and taking control of her own body. Really, what more is there to ask for?

If I were to go back three years and talk to my younger self, I would grab her by the shoulders, shake her really hard and ask her to start a dialogue. Make it raw and real and laughably uncomfortable. Sex is taboo because discomfort is feared. The act of normalizing uncomfortable topics is so valuable, and we as people do not bridge that gap enough. I'm guilty of it, and we are all probably guilty of it too.

We shame women for having sex, and men for not having sex, and that just makes no sense at all. It takes two to tango. These differing mindsets put unwanted critique and pressure on both ends of the spectrum. As a young person in general - most specifically a woman - we are on the cusp of owning our own sexuality. It's unbelievably detrimental to be shamed for something that we haven't even begun to fully explore ourselves. It breeds an unhealthy relationship with a truly beautiful and important part of life.

If I were to go back three years and talk to my younger self, I would tell her to talk to mom. Mom wants to know, she does. Mom doesn't need to know the details, but she'll find out eventually, so start the conversation. Sex education comes in all sorts of forms. From the classroom, from understanding yourself, and from having conversations about things that matter with the people who matter.

I get it. Kids don't want to think about their parents having sex and parents definitely don't want to think about their kids having sex. But by not talking about it, we breed a super toxic cycle of everybody knowing that it's happening (and most likely having questions) and nobody saying anything. Instead, it's time for the pendulum to swing and for dialogue to flow freely.

If I were to go back three years and talk to my younger self, I would tell her to throw the phrase "losing my virginity" straight out the window. This concept, frankly, is super fucked up. Even the way we phrase it is fucked up. What are we losing? After that night, I remember sitting on my couch and thinking that I didn't really feel like I lost anything. And I didn't. If anything we are gaining much more than we will ever lose. I was gaining a new experience, a new form of intimacy with another person.

Millennials as a generation are significantly more open-minded, creative and hungry for change than any other generation before us. Yet, these old colloquialized viewpoints of sex and shame still remain deeply rooted in everyday life. And now pop-culture presides as the driving force of sex education for today's youth- you can find just about anything on the internet, with the majority of Americans still consider sex a "private" matter.

There should be nothing private in a talk about privates. There is such an interesting dichotomy that emerges from this. In some ways, yes, it's good that there is that exposure out there, but it can often be sensationalized or falsified information that is detrimental to sex education as a whole. Answers to these questions should be readily available and come from a trustworthy source. If I were to go back three years and talk to my younger self, I would tell her to ask more questions. Ask them to people, not the internet, and ask them often.

I did not realize the importance of my sexual experiences until recently. And, at nineteen, I believe I am still discovering their magnitude every day. I didn't have a traumatic experience, nor do I feel that my family and friends would have openly shamed me for it, yet I still had that innate reaction to close up and pretend it didn't happen or that it wasn't a big deal. I think that's the root of the issue.

Even when the experiences are transformative and beautiful, the knee-jerk reaction is to keep it inside. I did not know about the nuances of sex enough to express my feelings about my own body. Ignorance is not bliss when it comes to all things sex. I wasn't even informed enough to recognize this was my mindset until significantly after the fact. Sex education should be more than learning how to put a condom on a wooden penis or statistics about STDs. While this is better than nothing, bare minimum sexual education should not be the standard of our system.

In Denmark, the sexual education curriculum has been entirely revolutionized. They open the dialogue starting as young as five. Ineke van der Vlugt, an expert on youth sexual development for Rutgers WPF, the Dutch sexuality research institute, has pioneered sexual education curriculums throughout the nation. "People often think we are starting right away to talk about sexual intercourse [with kindergartners]," van der Vlugt says. "Sexuality is so much more than that. It's also about self image, developing your own identity, gender roles, and it's about learning to express yourself, your wishes and your boundaries."[87] Sex happens. Sex happens a lot and in all sorts of different ways. Sex is fun. Everybody who has healthy sex knows that it is really fun. As long as it occurs between two consenting adults, have all the fun you want.

The purpose of a comprehensive sex education is not to encourage students to have sex. Although this may be what people assume, it instead fosters the idea that if young people want to have sex, then they deserve to be as informed as they possibly can be. It simply comes down to the idea of choice. Without the normalization of the topic, young people can't make the choice. The choice to do it, or not. The choice to be excited, or to keep it to ourselves. The choice to ask for help and be listened to, or stay quiet. These choices should be like second nature, not a wish or a hope.

I wonder what my choice would have been had 16-year-old me had the wisdom of present-day me. I wonder if the girl three seats down in math class asked her mom about sex, or if the sophomore boy on the soccer team got his information off the internet and secretly didn't know what was true and what was not. I wonder how that boy is doing, if he felt pressure or fear and didn't have enough information to be educated with regards to his choice. I wonder if the kids in Denmark know the wonderful knowledge they are gaining. I wonder what would have happened had 16-year-old me opened this very dialogue back then, something I have the power to do now.

We as Millennials are in the pivotal place to not just ask for the choice, but to demand it. Not to just ask for *some* sexual education, but insist that it is properly and extensively presented to the next generations. Our bodies, and the decisions we make with them, are so important. It is time to get comfortable with the uncomfortable and to start to insist on an open discussion about healthy sex. Those younger than us deserve the lessons we missed out on. We have the power to the deliver that to them. We are a generation of now, so let's get going.

DIY

What concrete steps can you take in the next year to achieve your goal?

ADEMILOLA OYETUGA

"For I know the plans I have for you" declares the Lord, "plans to prosper you and not to harm you, plans to give you hope and a future." ~ Jeremiah 29:1

Who am I?

My name is Ademilola Oyetuga and I am 20 years old. I am a first-generation Nigerian-American college student originally from Lakewood, Washington. I attend school across the country, in upstate NY, so that I can gain more independence and experience a completely new culture. I am a neuroscience major on the pre-med track, and I aspire to work in the healthcare field so that I can be a role model for kids not offered the same opportunities.

What world do I want to live In?

I want to live in a world where diversity is celebrated, a world where music can be shared, languages can be spoken and learned, and cultures can flourish. I want to live in a world where we are all recognized as human beings, each made to be perfectly unique and able to be our authentic selves.

I want to live in a world where all people are given the opportunity to have access to good education and healthcare not because it is a luxury, but because it is essential and should be a right.

I want to live in a world where I no longer have to wake up and recognize that I am black and a woman. I want to live in a world where my present and future are not based off of tragedies of the past.

What is a character trait that you wish you could change in yourself?

Control. Control has manifested itself in my life in the most random ways. For one, my desire to have control has made me a strong leader, a reliable and loyal friend, and fiercely independent. On the other hand, control has made me strong-willed/ hard-headed, and sensitive about minimal things.

When I am in control, I feel as if nothing can hurt me. I can manage all the variables in a situation and find the best method of approach. It took me a long time to accept this key characteristic in myself because I was aware of the bad things associated with it. I was afraid that people would say that I am a perfectionist with no clear path, or that they would realize that I do not have all of the answers. I like the way it feels when people need me, and I feared that I would become useless to others if they knew the truth. I let these untrue fears prevent me from feeling free from myself and too dependent on what others thought of me instead of what I thought of myself.

There is always a positive and negative effect to some things, and control is no different. In the process of changing how much power control has on my life, I want to learn how to be more spontaneous, to live in the moment, and to genuinely trust that all will be well in the future.

Why is social change such an important issue, especially today having so much information available all the time?

In my eyes, social change should be positive and beneficial to the society it affects. With that being said, social change is an important issue because without it there would be no such thing as progress or equality. Without social change, as an African American woman, I would be essentially irrelevant to society today. There are so many injustices in the world, and without people taking action to fix the problems, they will persist.

Although I believe that social change is the key to a better and more equal future, for every supporter of change there is a non-supporter. I think that people choose to prevent social change out of fear of losing key privileges that support their economic, political, or social goals. However, people forget that providing equal opportunities to a marginalized group does not mean decreasing the quality or quantity of what the un-marginalized group has. When there is equality for all, everyone benefits.

The Ones Left Behind:
How America is Failing the Poor

Ademilola Oyetuga

Stop. Inhale. Focus. Exhale. Open your mind.

The statistics are well known. They have been thrown around for years upon years now. The United States, although one of the wealthiest countries in the world, is also one of the most unequal countries in regards to wealth distribution. The unequal distribution of wealth among Americans is as follows: in 2016, the top 1% of families controlled 38.6% of the country's wealth, which is almost twice as much as the bottom 90% of families, who hold about 22.8% of the wealth.[88] The wealth distribution is so unequal that rich people are not as wealthy as they should be, and everyone ranging from the middle class to the lower class is suffering due to the skewed levels of inequality. However, this is nothing new. The problem has been identified, but what is needed is a solution.

So let's look at the possible solutions: increase availability and affordability of financial services, decrease unemployment, support pay equity, and increase minimum wage. There are plenty of possible solutions to the issue of poverty, but even when these ideas are taken into consideration by government officials and are actually applied, the problem still persists. What other solution could there be?

Now, think about a child you know. A tiny human that is too young, too innocent, and too naive to know the challenges of life. A child living in blissful ignorance, their dreams circling with endless possibility. Imagine being as free as a child with nothing but hope, courage, and opportunity to look forward to. Smiling, because, well, why not? Loving, because hate is a foreign concept. Free.

Are you jealous yet? This is childhood, or at least what childhood should be like for everyone…

The name of the girl in this scenario has been changed to conceal her identity.

Alicia was a close friend of mine in 5th grade, and the following scenario represents the conversations I overheard between her and her mother as she would pick us up for soccer practice. How familiar does this sound?:

> Parent: Hey, bud! How was school today?
>
> Alicia: It was great!
>
> Parent: Tell me all about it.
>
> Alicia: Well, first we went over our homework, and then our science teacher bought a bunch of playdough and toothpicks for us to create the planets in the solar system. After that, we ate carrots and hummus for snack and had recess. After recess, we did reading and math, and we met up with Ms. Jones. She is awesome.
>
> Parent: Ms. Jones? Who is she?
>
> Alicia: She is the school counselor! She said that if we need help with anything we can talk to her. She also has the best chocolates in her office…. Oh and can you sign this permission slip for school?
>
> Parent: What's it for?
>
> Alicia: We are going to the history museum next week with Mr. Cecade. He said that because we have been so good, he'll bring in some

cupcakes for us too! Oh, and in a few weeks we are going to have another field trip to the zoo, where we will meet a real veterinarian!

Parent: That is so nice! I am happy you are enjoying school. Do you have homework?

Alicia: Yeah, I do. I'm excited to do it.

Parent: I am sure you are, bud, but first let's get you to soccer practice. I'll sign that slip later.

Compare the first scenario to this one. The name of this girl has been changed for her protection. Jaimee is a girl I recently met while volunteering at an organization similar to the Boys and Girls Club:

Me: Hey Jaimee! How was school today? I want to know everything.

Jaimee: It was okay I guess… my teacher yelled at me again…

Me: Why did your teacher yell at you?

Jaimee: Because he thought that I was being disrespectful by talking, but I was just trying to tell my friend to stop talking. I tried to explain that to him, but he just got angrier and said I was lying…

Me: Wow, I'm sorry Jaimee. That really sucks. How did that make you feel?

Jaimee: I got really angry, but I can't do anything about it. This happens to everyone, so it is no big deal I guess.

Me: Alright, well I am sorry you had to go through this. Is there any homework that I can help you with?

Jaimee: No. None of my teachers give us homework anymore because they know that no one will do it. They just gave up.

Me: What? But you are in fifth grade! You have to have homework to do. Don't you want to learn?

Jaimee: Yeah, but oh well. Do your teachers ever not give you homework?

Mc: No. We always have assignments. Well, what do you want to do? Go over some math?

Jaimee: No thanks. I'd rather just go upstairs and read a book.

Me: What book?

Jaimee: Have you heard of Frankenstein? I am almost

done with it!

Me: Okay cool Jaimee, I will come back to check on you later...

What is it that Alicia has that Jaimee is missing? For one, Alicia comes from a wealthy middle-class family living in a high-income neighborhood. Her family had enough money to send her to a private school, thus giving her access to quality education where the teachers care about the students rather than give up on them. She was constantly being inspired and motivated to continue her education, to reach for the stars and enter a career field of her choice. She was being led along a pre-destined track to receive a college education, which will in turn help her make statistically over $15,000 more than a high school graduate.[89]

Alicia went through a lot as a child: the divorce of her parents, the death of loved ones, anxiety, depression, and self-hate. Alicia did not have the perfect childhood and was forced to grow up much too soon, but she did have the benefit of not having to worry about her education or pursing her professional dreams.

There are many kids like Alicia in the world, but what about Jaimee? Kids like Jaimee, who come from low income families, represent the majority of public school students in the U.S.[90] These kids are subjected to this lifestyle because of their socioeconomic status and because of where they live. In almost every case, the kids receiving the worst education are those coming from low income families. There is a clear correlation between education and socioeconomic status, but I believe that one problem, education, can be the solution to an even greater problem: poverty.

There are plenty of factors that contribute to the quality of an education a child receives. Here in the US, the quality can be most readily attributed to the portion of tax revenue a public school receives from local property taxes, which in turn amplifies the difference between high-income and low-income neighborhoods. To put it simply: the better the neighborhood, the better the education. For a public school education, it costs approximately $10,615 on average per kid,[91] with the majority of public schools paying less than this value.

Due to the shift to a majority poor population of students and public schools paying less money per child, kids entering kindergarten start off already behind and are rarely able to catch up to their more privileged peers. These kids are less likely to have family support at home, less likely to be exposed to extracurricular or enriching activities outside of school, more likely to drop out, and, ultimately, less likely to pursue higher education. Without a college degree, how are these kids supposed to progress in life and climb up the socio-economic ladder? How can they find a job that allows them to support their families and also receive benefits like health and dental insurance, which are luxuries out of reach for those living in poverty today?

Education has a significant influence on poverty, but it is important to note that poverty also affects how someone learns. To be able to really learn, one must be actively present, but when one doesn't know where one's next meal is coming from or when one's next shower will be, how can one focus on reading *Little House on the Prairie* or *To Kill a Mockingbird*?

Speaking to the strong relation between education and poverty, Michael A. Rebell of the Campaign for Educational Equity at Teachers College at Columbia University emphasized that, "We have to give [our students] quality teachers, small class sizes, up-to-date equipment. But in addition, if we're serious, we have to do things that overcome the damages of poverty. We have to meet their health needs, their mental health needs, after-school programs, summer programs, parent engagement, early-childhood services. These are the so-called wraparound services. Some people think of them as add-ons. They're not. They're imperative."[92] By doing these things, the cycle of poverty can be broken and new levels of achievement and opportunity can be gained.

Jaimee is in a tough situation right now, but I am afraid to say that she is better off than many. What I did not mention earlier is that Jaimee is white, and in the United States today, being white automatically gives Jaimee a leg up on non-Asian minority students.

Demographically, African American and Hispanic people make up the largest population living in poverty in the United States. They are also the ones left behind in more ways than one. In life, it is hard to avoid crime, and living in poverty makes that task even harder. As a result, they desperately turn to crime as a last resort. It is evident that non-Asian people of color are unfairly treated by the justice system and have been since the formation of the United States. The numbers do not lie. In 2014, African-Americans made up 2.3 million (34%) of the total 6.8 million correctional population. African Americans are incarcerated at more than five times the rate of white people. African American women are imprisoned two times the rate of white women. Across the United States, African American children represent 32% of children who are arrested, 42% of children who are detained, and 53% of children whose cases brought up in criminal court. Lastly, even though African Americans and Hispanics make up about 32% of the United States population, they comprise 56% of all incarcerated people in 2015.[93]

Just as education is related to poverty, it is impossible to exclude the power that race has over both domains. Feeding into the mass incarceration of primarily African American men in the United States are our education institutes. A term that we like to call the "school to prison pipeline" accentuates the disproportional tendency of disadvantaged/low-income children who are incarcerated or entering the juvenile or criminal justice system due to harsh school policies. This "pipeline" draws attention to the lack of resources available for students -- overcrowded classrooms, the lack of qualified and well-paid teachers, and insufficient funds for school counselors and advisors, special education services, textbook acquisition, extracurricular opportunities, and so on. Without these resources, students are more likely to drop out.

Even worse, some teachers actually encourage their students to drop out because of the pressure from test-based accountability policies, such as the "No Child Left Behind" act. Unfortunately, the "pipeline" often includes a "zero-tolerance policy" that criminalizes minor infractions within the school. This ultimately leads to higher levels of suspension and expulsion, putting students in the fast-track lane leading directly to the juvenile justice system. Suspension and/or expulsion leads students to be left unsupervised more often than not, and easily helps students fall behind in their school work (which feeds the dropout levels). To make matters worse, when schools become places where students have to stand in line to walk through metal detectors, and where hallways are patrolled by officers rather than school officials, they become more like cold and dehumanized prisons than warm and welcoming places for learning.

Especially for kids, the environment in which they live, or at least spend a significant amount of time, directly affects the type of person they will become in the future. The "pipeline" psychologically normalizes this negative environment, thus effectively closing off more hopeful and constructive pathways.[94] Poverty, race, and education are all intertwined. It is impossible to solve one without addressing them all. So what can we do to support our kids?

I think that people are afraid to lose what they have, what they have earned, and what they want; and any form of change directly puts these values at risk. However, when it comes to the marginalization of a particular class or race, change that promotes equality traditionally is mutually beneficial—when groups support each other, they become stronger and better off than they were before. Within the United States, if we all work together to end poverty and racial achievement differences, then we can flourish. A way in which the divide is being mended is by simply proving opportunities.

Affirmative Action, for example, provides under-represented and often low income students with employment and educational opportunities that have historically been denied. Although there are some issues surrounding Affirmative Action (reverse discrimination, biased...etc), it does represent a step forward to providing equality. There is no such thing as a perfect solution.

I myself am a beneficiary of opportunity programs. As an African American woman from a lower middle class family, paying for college was my biggest struggle. We were not poor enough to receive most forms of aid, but not wealthy enough to afford a college education without aid.

I was accepted at Union College through its Academic Opportunity Program (AOP), an extension of the Higher Education Opportunity Program (HEOP) for New York state residents. This program helps economically and educationally disadvantaged students obtain forms of higher education, but to be honest, many of these programs do much more than that. The program specific to Union College provides personal support as well, which is something I truly value.

College is an experience of a lifetime, but the road is not always easy. There have been plenty of times I thought about dropping out —the pressure and the stress of college take their toll— but the thought of how many other students could have taken my place is a constant reminder to seize opportunities while I can.

AOP has provided me with the resources to pursue my career dreams. This program has helped take the burden off of my shoulders so that I can focus on my academics and college experiences. Having that constant reaffirmation that I can succeed, and having a space, group of friends and advisors that I can turn to about literally anything in my life has been the most impactful and meaningful part of my college experience thus far. Union College's opportunity program is a strong reminder of the benefits that come from providing disadvantaged students with quality education. My peers in the program, along with myself, are primarily in leadership roles on campus and also have a higher graduation rate than Union College itself.

Programs like AOP follow the mission of the similarly impactful Posse Foundation, which "is rooted in the belief that a small, diverse group of talented students—a Posse— carefully selected and trained, can serve as a catalyst for individual and community development. As the United States becomes an increasingly multicultural society, Posse believes that the leaders of the 21st century should reflect the country's rich demographic mix. The key to a promising future for our nation rests on the ability of strong leaders from diverse backgrounds to develop consensus solutions to complex social problems."[95] These two educational opportunities are developing the leaders of tomorrow by bridging the educational divide within the United States. This in turn helps lift youth out of low-income environments. In no way have these opportunity programs negatively affected more privileged people, showing how helping everyone provides greater equality.

So what is next? What can we do to make these changes happen? We can start in your own neighborhood. If we can better our neighborhoods, then we can better the schools within those districts. To do that we can address local officials and make sure that no matter what, every child will have the opportunity to receive a quality education. Teachers who do not support kids or are simply unqualified to teach need to be removed, and administrators who would rather depend on officers to criminalize students should also be removed.

Another way to help resolve this problem is to support student aid advocacy day, a day when students, faculty, opportunity program administrators, higher education policy makers, and legislators come together to promote higher education and ensure that student aid budgets are not cut. Above all, is important for children to have role models who look like them, sound like them, and exemplify what they could be in the future. Students who have benefitted from opportunity programs need to come back to their schools to motivate student, who are now in their shoes, to not give up. They also need to spread the word to younger children so that they are aware of how much opportunity is available to them.

The greatest gift we can give our children is hope. We need to start standing up for what is right and what is wrong, rather than let our kids get pushed aside by the system to be forgotten once again.

HAYDEN PANETH

Who am I?

I am a first generation college student, and the oldest of my parents' nine children. I love my family just as much as I value my 'alone time'. I am strong-minded, yet guided by my soft heart. Once I graduate college I aspire to become the parent of a large dog.

How do I see myself as a changemaker?

I see myself as a changemaker by living my best life. When people see my heart and hear my story they are inspired by their own strengths and resilience. For me, the time is always right to do the right thing.

What world do I want to live In?

My ideal world is one where every human being has access to education, a supportive social circle, and superlative health care.

Why is social change so important?

Social change is important to me because as a society we are inadvertently influencing one another. Since every human being has power over their own decisions, we can create a ripple effect just by doing the right thing for ourselves.

The Crossed Out, Torn Out Pages

Hayden Paneth

Preface

Sharing the story of the first 18 years of my life has been hard. I despise talking about it. The process of writing about how I was mistreated at home, in my community, and in school brings about painful memories. I was so lost, alone, and hated myself. I could not understand what I had done to be completely isolated from a world that I have come to know as loving, freeing, and full of opportunities.

My journey out of the Hasidic community was frightening. I would cry all the time. I knew that I wanted to live a life free of isolation, but I did not know a single person outside of the Hasidic community. There was no one to share the fear of being a suicide statistic, or the joy of scoring in the top 5th percentile of GED test scores. The raw emotions I experienced writing this part of my life's story will be worth the anguish as long as one child in the Hasidic community believes that they too deserve a fair and free education.

I heard the echo of Mommy's determined footsteps approaching my bedroom. I was on the top bunk-bed, my sister on the bottom. I had already stopped adjusting my sleeping position, feet curled under my patterned blanket. Both my sister and I were reading a book - the light was still on in our bedroom. Mommy's footsteps continued as she circled around the door, squeezing by the white metal bunk to turn off the light. She was about to flip the switch when I sat up abruptly. I wanted to look at Mommy's face as I was going to tell her something. "I want to attend a better school,"

I blurted out in a fast, but pleading tone. Mommy's hand flew off the light switch and her body turned to face me. Like a deer caught in bright headlights she looked at me with her beautiful brown eyes. I could see the conundrum of emotions in them, yet I knew Mommy well enough to anticipate her response. After a moment that felt like forever, her hand reached upward as the room went dark. I could not see her eyes anymore. I only heard her body slipping past the metal bars of the bed as she exited my room taking my agency with her.

The next morning my body awakened to the sun pouring through the space between the shade and the window frame in my small, square shaped bedroom. I spread my cover neatly over my flattened pillow, and then, covered the entire mattress. Placing the soles of my feet carefully onto the ladder I made my way down till I felt the roughness of the once shined parquet floors. I curved my spine bending over to wash *Negal Vassar* (nail water) that was prepared the night before. It is a ritual all ultra-Orthodox families take part in every morning after waking up, to clean our hands from the impurity of sleep. Observance of rituals were the biggest part of my life, something that separated me from those that did not observe. I lifted the *Negal Vassar* while water was still dripping from my hands and dropped the pail at once into the bathtub.

Negel Vasser, modesty, and pre-breakfast prayers, are some of the guidelines implemented in Hasidic households. My firmly-pressed uniform jumper swished as I slipped it over my face. I pulled the jumper all the way below my knees and alas, every inch, from my collar bone to my toes, were covered.

The prayers were like the monotonic chanting of a grasshopper. To the untrained ear the words all sounded the same, but we understood our intentions as we prayed. My siblings and I fervently recited our pre-breakfast prayers, taking turns answering "Amen" after every blessing. There was barely any time to eat before my sisters and I hopped onto the rowdy bus that honked in front of our house.

Our ride had our school's name printed in black bold Hebrew letters. It drove down the block, around the corner, stopping and driving around the streets of Borough Park, Brooklyn. The city that never sleeps houses a community which prefers social and religious isolation.

Looking out the window of my yellow school bus, the activity was nothing like the mélange that is within Manhattan, just a short 13.3 miles from Borough Park. In my city, the streets are wide but the houses are close together. The abundance of popular culture so present in New York City does not trickle into my world. Instead, mothers sit on doorsteps surrounded by children, bikes, and baby carriages. Men in black garments are seen walking rapidly, as their wet side curls dangle with the motion of their steps.

The noise on the bus quieted down as it pulled up in front of the beige stucco, block-wide school building. My body peeled off the black leather bus seat and I moved toward the front of the bus.

The three mile radius I grew up in contains at least fifteen private all-girls' schools. While there are public schools in the vicinity, ultra-Orthodox Hasidic parents send their daughters to an educational institution in which Yiddish studies are taught in intricate depth. Secular studies such as Math, Science, Biology, and Grammar are taught just enough to cover the basics. Yiddish studies consist of the laws of *Shabbos*, *Tznius* (modesty), Yiddish grammar and writing. Subjects like these are of utmost importance for Hasidic girls because they have a special life mission and school is geared to prepare them for it.

In Hasidic families, the common belief is that each child has their own *tafkid* (purpose) they were sent down to accomplish on this earth. In families like mine, a boy is groomed to learn *Torah*, study the *Talmud*, and spend day and night as an adult understanding the teachings of our revered forefathers. In order to accomplish this, young boys attend yeshiva where they are taught Torah studies from Sunday until Friday.

Just like the boys, the content of education plays an integral role in preparing Hasidic girls for adult life. In Satmar girls school, I was taught how to fulfill my god-given *tafkid* of being a revered wife to my future husband. I knew from a very young age that being a devout wife and becoming a mother was the most important mission I can accomplish in my life. While I was young, I somehow knew this was to be my destiny, just as it was my mother's.

English is my second language. It was taught to me and my fellow classmates when we were in the first grade. Mastering the ABC's was easy since at that time I was able to read and write in Yiddish and Hebrew. While Satmar school did teach me how to read, write, and speak the English language, I did not know that they deliberately avoided subjects such as Algebra, Physics, Chemistry, Coding, Biology to be part of the curriculum. Most importantly, they failed to encourage my growth as an independent thinker. My school teaches its students just enough to provide a substantially equivalent education compared to public schools. The books used by us students are provided by the government. What the government does not know is that these books are heavily censored.

The irony of a community that did not use birth control and encouraged parents to have as many children as possible, tearing out the endocrine system in biology books, was lost on me. But, the natural curiosity I possessed inside, the deep desire to increase my knowledge, collided with the crossed out, torn out pages in my textbooks.

I remember that day vividly, as if I had just experienced it. That day, while my modern Orthodox neighbors and I were playing outdoors, they said to me, "The school you attend teaches English subjects that are lower than your grade level." I was confused. I knew that my neighbors had more freedom and exposure to the secular world than I did: they are allowed to watch movies, something that is forbidden in my family. Talking to the male population is considered okay for my neighbors, while we are not supposed to be seen or heard by men. They eat out at Kosher restaurants in Boro Park, while we enjoyed food cooked at home. They conversed in English at home; we spoke Yiddish only. We used to answer the bell with "Who's there," but then Totty (father) said that whoever does not understand Yiddish does not enter our home. From that day on, we answer the doorbell in my mother tongue, "Ver is dort?"

While the children were still praying, I began my journey of disobeying. I was too curious, too determined to simply follow the rules. A resolve to learn overtook my heart. While most teenagers around the world fell in love with human beings, I fell in love with education. I found creative and perhaps almost scandalous ways of attaining books to read. Since the public library and English books were off-limits, I used my modern Orthodox neighbors as resources. During my late teens, I spent days in their basements and sleepless nights on my bunk bed gulping literary knowledge.

Soon, the resources ran out. There were no more books to read. A spark occurred. A novel, frightening thought. College. Just the thought of it sent a shiver through my slender modest self.

While my classmates were getting engaged to be married, I explored my options. I showed up to Brooklyn College with modest attire but uncharted joy to take classes for the GED. I could not use my high school diploma since it lacked the most basic courses colleges require. For three months, I took those courses. I now had access to internet and began looking into colleges. The little girl inside me never imagined that my desire to go to a better school would be answered in the form of a college acceptance letter.

The Hasidic community is not just a culture of people who dress as if they lived in ancient Europe, pray, and educate their children differently. They are gifted and talented, but deny their children basic educational freedom. Among the many children, adults and rabbinical leaders, there is a child just like me: a child who yearns for agency, a child who wishes to read a book in bright sunlight. It is up to the ones who understand the freedom that an education can provide, to advocate for those children. The Hasidic education is meaningful and important. But so is allowing children to learn that which can enrich their personal identity. I have not been as happy as I am now since I was six-years-old. This is because I have grown as a person in this vast world of knowledge.

It is with my personal story that I call political, social, and religious leaders to action. As a child of the Hasidic school system the veil has to be lifted. Get to know the children instead of the ones in charge of their education. In a country that is proud of religious and personal freedom, there is enough room for personal freedom while not tainting their religious identity. Speak to them, advocate for their rights. Say the words they mean to say but don't know how. This is about no more crossed out, torn out pages of their textbooks.

What You Can Do

Young Advocates for Fair Education (YAFFED), is an organization that advocates for the fair education of Hasidic Children. Sharing this story with friends, completing an internship, or donating could allow this organization to continue its work. I have advocated alongside YAFFED to get the government to enforce Hasidic schools to educate their young. Had an organization like YAFFED been around when I was going through school, perhaps the pages in my book would not have been crossed out.

DIY

Create your own "call to action" that gives your mission direction for further development.

KATHLEEN SINATRA

"The only person you are destined to become is the person you decide to be." ~ Ralph Waldo Emerson

Who am I?

I am a first year student at Union College, born in 1999, from Bridgewater, CT. While undeclared, I am interested in studying Political Science and Spanish. I am involved in extracurriculars that focus on diversity and community service, and am a tour guide on campus.

What does changemaker mean to you?

Being a changemaker means actively participating in a social change movement that betters society. However, I think in order to be an effective changemaker, one must not simply participate in the movement, but garner support by communicating why it is important to aid in this change.

Why is social change such an important issue, especially with so much information available all the time?

I think that social change is especially important because of our ability to access an unprecedented amount of information. Not only can we find out about a topic in a matter of seconds, but we are constantly exposed to information through social media, simultaneously allowing us to utilize social media to advertise and support social change movements. As such, not acting upon information that pertains to necessary social change makes us passive members of our global community.

What world do I want to live in?

I want to live in a world that is kind. I want to live in a world that is peaceful. I feel as though these are two goals that often seem impossible to achieve. And, while this may be true, I think that it all starts at a place of acceptance. Whether that be acceptance of religious differences or political perspectives, I would like to see a world that embraces differences and does not fear or persecute them. Should we be able to begin a dialogue that allows for this, I believe we can begin to reach these seemingly utopian ideas.

"But you look fine!": Navigating High School with an Invisible, Chronic Illness

Kathleen Sinatra

Part I: If Only It Were Tattooed on My Forehead

I was 12 years old, and I could not get out of bed. My peers were playing soccer, going to the movies, having sleepovers, and I could barely accomplish a few hours of school work on a good day.

I remember the exact weekend I first became sick. I slept for three days straight, only waking up for meals. We all assumed it was some sort of virus. I would feel better soon. I spent the next six years struggling with what turned out to be chronic Lyme disease and Bartonella, a co-infection. I developed symptoms of intense headaches, an extreme sore throat, and aching joints, but the fatigue was the worst. It was constant and unending.

"I don't understand. When I see Kathleen in school, she looks fine. When I ask her how she is, she says she is okay." This was what an administrator said to my parents. I had been sick for a year and had just found out that my initial diagnosis of mononucleosis was a false positive. I was in a constant state of medical limbo. I was frustrated and scared. And this is what she chose to say. The comment was well-intentioned. But the unintentional ignorance rang hollow to me.

Humans understand only what is tangible. We crave the ability to see it, to touch it, to know that it is real. Without this ability, we often question its reality. The problem with invisible illnesses is that it is just that - invisible. You will not be able to see it. It has no face. Accepting it is hard, for both you, as the observer, and me, as the one with the illness. There were many instances where I wished my illness was visible, that it were tattooed on my forehead so that one could see and know how much I was struggling. Because without this, I felt like I needed to prove I was sick. But how can you even do that?

When you see someone with a cast, you do not question the validity of their diagnosis, symptoms, or necessary accommodations. But just because you can't see it, doesn't make it is less real. I knew that the pounding headaches were real. I knew that the never-ending fatigue was real. I knew that I was sick. I know you can't see it, but I know that it is real.

My response of "I'm fine" or "I'm okay" was my best attempt to be positive. It amazed me that my positivity somehow seemed to invalidate my illness to them. I had essentially given up all the things I enjoyed: swimming, soccer, spending time with friends, only to become a slave to my bed. I was a teenager who was supposed to be having fun, yet I was trapped in my own, failing body. But, dwelling on this would have only been more destructive.

Did they really want or expect me to respond, "I feel horrible. I am so fatigued I could crumble, but I have pushed with everything I have to get myself here." Had I always been honest with how I felt, nobody would have wanted to be around me. My answer would not have been what they wanted. The dichotomy between feeling that I had to validate that I was sick, yet feeling as though they didn't actually want to hear about it, was toxic. Trying my best to be positive was what I could control. This was my life. And while it was not fun, I had to hold onto hope and happiness. I had no power over how I felt, but I did have power over my mindset.

Part II: A Problem Greater than Me

Chronic Lyme disease is controversial within the medical community. Some contend that, while a debilitating illness, its effects are only temporary. With a treatment of a few weeks worth of antibiotics, symptoms should only last anywhere from a few weeks to a few months. To them, chronic Lyme disease is not real. But, this is not what many have experienced. This was certainly not what I experienced. I was sick for six years. And I struggled with Lyme every day for those six years.

Because of the division within the medical community over the existence of chronic Lyme, garnering support is more difficult. Support is also affected by the lack of knowledge surrounding the exact number of people suffering from chronic Lyme disease. Trying to figure out the exact number of people with this illness is best exemplified through a Google search. Type in "chronic Lyme disease" and you will get varying numbers ranging from 160,000 to 19,000,000 results. Regardless of the number, you will find thousands of articles that talk about changes that need to occur in terms of testing, how to best treat chronic Lyme, but perhaps most importantly, articles and blogs that detail the struggles of those who deal with chronic Lyme.

Skye Cowie, a nineteen year old professional freestyle soccer player shares, "My only relief was in sleep. I had no social life. Worse, perhaps, was that I had no friends who understood what I was going through. Getting up for school and faking a smile to hide my suffering had become impossible."[96]

Christina Kovacs, creator of the blog Lady of Lyme, writes that "When someone has been healthy all their lives they can't possibly understand what it's like to be sick 24/7. It feels like every day is a new hurdle to climb, a new symptom to try and manage, and a new explanation to give to the world. I don't have the time nor the energy to explain to each person individually what I go through on a daily basis."[97]

Amy Tan, noted author and co-founder of LymeAid 4 Kids, says, "Worst of all, I could not read a paragraph and recall what it said. I wrote in circles, unable to tie two thoughts together, nevermind the plot of a novel. Yet, outwardly, I looked normal — just a bit listless and tired, at times apathetic then overly emotional. The doctors I saw — excellent ones — never considered testing me for Lyme disease, even though I suggested it once. "Very rare," one said, "and not in California." More than four years later, in 2003, I finally found a doctor familiar with the disease. Three months after antibiotic treatment, I could write again."[98]

These are just three out of the hundreds of articles written by or about people who deal with chronic Lyme disease. Although the medical community doesn't know the precise number of sufferers, it has become clear that the numbers are significant. It forces me to realize that my story is just one of thousands. It is not a story of me; it is a story of us. And, it is bigger than chronic Lyme disease. Lupus. Crohn's Disease. Arthritis. Mental Illnesses. This list could go on. These are the unseen illnesses that affect a large number of people, yet so many of our voices are not heard, and we remain overlooked.

Part III: What Must Change

I struggled with chronic Lyme the entirety of my high school education. As such, I know that there are clear changes that could be made in the high school education system when dealing with students who struggle with invisible illnesses, like Lyme Disease. They would not only significantly benefit students, but benefit administrators and educators alike.

The U.S. Department of Education states that, "The Section 504 regulations require a school district to provide a 'free appropriate public education' (FAPE) to each qualified student with a disability who is in the school district's jurisdiction, regardless of the nature or severity of the disability. Under Section 504, FAPE consists of the provision of regular or special education and related aids and services designed to meet the student's individual educational needs as adequately as the needs of non-disabled students are met."[99]

I realize that meeting the needs of students is not easy. My father is a high school English teacher, and I know that it is a profession that is challenging and sometimes unappreciated. As a teacher you have multiple classes a day and are given little time to prepare, as such, catering to the individual needs of students is difficult. Furthermore, explains Lisa Holmes, a high school special education teacher, "students who are afforded a 504 under the Americans With Disabilities Act, when there is a medical diagnosis attached to the disability do not fall under the responsibility of special education teachers. This makes it the duty of regular education teachers to deal with the needs of the student." This can be understandably frustrating and overwhelming for teachers.

But it is essential that as an educator you remember it is your job to fairly educate each student to the best of your ability. Just like a learning disability or a physical disability, chronic and invisible illnesses are devastating and should be approached by the education system as deserving of the same type of attention. They too are a disability.

To recognize chronic Lyme as a disability was difficult for some of the educators at my school. To those that struggle with understanding, I say this: you would never ask a person with a broken leg to run a mile. If, for some reason, it were essential that they complete this mile, you would no doubt accommodate them. You would understand that they would require additional time. You would see that, in order to make the playing field as level as possible, other accommodations might be needed.

This is the mentality with which one must approach invisible illnesses. I was not like my peers. I was struggling with a chronic illness and, just like the person completing the mile with a broken leg, I too needed extra support to finish the tasks.

So how does a school determine what accommodations should be put in place? This is the question. And, to be honest, there is no clear-cut answer. Symptoms, as well as severity, can vary from person to person. As such, accommodation plans must be personalized.

Before falling ill, I was unaware of my options. What I learned is that the ways in which a student can be accommodated is innumerable. For example, my processing abilities, which were affected by the Lyme, impacted the speed of my reading and writing. With my energy already very limited, addressing this specific problem proved helpful. A special education teacher was assigned and she read aloud to me and transcribed my work. In addition, I was taught to use online tools to complete work at home. There were certainly other ways in which this could have been addressed, but this was what was most effective for me. Just like with treatment, there is no cookie cutter accommodation plan for students with chronic Lyme, or other chronic and invisible illnesses.

A student accommodation plan will evolve and change. How I was feeling changed over my four years of high school, so the ways in which I needed help also changed. My freshman year I was homebound, but by my senior year, I was essentially a full time student. I went from requiring major adjustments in terms of the work, having a special education teacher come to my house every day, to having a free period that allowed me extra rest and extensions for work as needed. But, even within a school year, my accommodations changed based on my health. When it comes to accommodations and tackling invisible and chronic illnesses, it is important to be flexible, creative, and willing to try out different approaches. As soon as something is not working, change it. If you need more help, ask for it.

For the future, I wish for professional development about chronic Lyme. Expert knowledge and educational information to educate teachers and administrators would be helpful. In doing so, they will learn about how chronic Lyme disease affects students and how to best approach an education care plan. This is especially important since 504 students remain the duty of regular education teachers. Without professional development supported by guidance or administration, how are teachers meant to know how to accommodate these students? Without this support for teachers, both staff and students are left without critical assistance.

The final step, pertinent to the success of all of the other steps listed above, is communication. Asking for help was probably the most difficult skill for me to learn. I did not want to need extra time to complete assignments. I did not want to have to get tutoring. I did not want to ever feel like a burden. I did not want to feel different.

I tried my best to communicate with teachers, knowing that the strongest advocate for me was myself, but learning to do this was challenging (especially when I didn't feel well). I was a teenager being asked to communicate to adults how I was feeling with an illness that sometimes affected me differently day by day. I also was not a special education teacher trained on accommodations and did not know what would help or was even in the realm of possibilities. So, not wanting to acknowledge that I needed help, and then lacking the knowledge in terms of ways my school could help me, made it even more of a challenge.

I remember the day one teacher called me "flippant" and said that I should be more "proactive" in terms of getting work done. Or when another told me that she didn't understand why I needed help. Being vulnerable and speaking with my teachers about something deeply personal was already uncomfortable and difficult for me. Then, fearing an aggressive or unpleasant reaction from a teacher only made communicating that much more difficult.

For students with Lyme and other chronic illnesses to best be aided, there should be communication beyond the student and teacher. My parents were very active in trying to help me, bridging contact between my doctors and the school, emailing administrators to set up meetings, consulting with disability advocates, basically doing everything in their power to help. But my parents were not in school with me and they were not in charge of educating me. And other sufferers might not have parental support at all.

There must be communication between the student and teacher, but also teacher to teacher and teacher to administrator. For this to occur, there must be a contact person available to the student that oversees the accommodation plan. The key word here is "availability." Insistent that this would help, I was assigned a special education teacher to my case. She was able to communicate to teachers how I felt, validating to them that what I was experiencing was real and also coming up with ideas on how to best aid me. Without her, I would not have made it through high school.

Lastly, I would strongly encourage students dealing with chronic and invisible illnesses to meet with a therapist or counselor. It is not uncommon for those struggling with chronic illness to also deal with anxiety and depression as a result of their illness. Addressing these problems is crucial. I was incredibly resistant to seeing a therapist, and the only way my parents got me to go was by bribing me with an iPhone (no joke). I had this very warped idea that by accepting help from a therapist I was somehow weak. But, I wasn't weak, I was just sick.

Going to therapy was the best decision I ever made. Having worked with students dealing with chronic and invisible illnesses before, my therapist had knowledge about accommodations that might help. But perhaps most importantly, she was able to help me accept what was happening to me. She recognized the difficulties I faced - health-wise, academically, and emotionally - and helped me work through them.

Part IV: Today and the Future

I am now eighteen years old and in college. After six years, I finally feel healthy. While I still have days where I don't feel as well, I now know that I simply have to rest. I make sacrifices in terms of my diet, and I am probably the only college student that likes to be in bed by 10pm. But, I have not felt this well since sixth grade.

Students should not have to go through what I experienced. The education system must make changes so as to better support us. They must recognize that chronic and invisible illnesses are a disability. Empowering and supporting educators through professional development is crucial. This informs them about students illnesses and how they can best aid them. They must be open and willing to communicate. And, most importantly for the community of people who suffer from invisible and chronic illnesses, my hope is that we can encourage sufferers to speak out and serve as role models for those who can't. So nobody will have to hear "but you look fine" again.

Resources

The U.S Department of Education information on protecting students with disabilities: https://www2.ed.gov/about/offices/list/ocr/504faq.html#introduction

Information on Lyme Disease:
International Lyme and Associated Diseases Society (ILADS): http://www.ilads.org/
Global Lyme Alliance: https://globallymealliance.org/

Generation Now: Millennials Call for Social Change

EPILOGUE

Continue The Wave

On a cold, wintery afternoon we collected our belongings and headed in a single file onto a small bus provided by our college. At that time, we thought we had chosen to take an ordinary Writing Across Curriculum course at Union College. The wheels started turning, driving down the street. Turning corners, stopping at red lights, in no time we had arrived. The room looked nothing like a classroom, but more like an office space for professionals. Instead of ordinary walls, we were surrounded by tall, thick windows. The aperture's flat surface was perfect for writing in washable markers. And so, while the cold sun was above us, the journey of Millennials writing a book brought us together.

On that very first day of our "Millennials and Social Change" class, a personal narrative began to form within us. The colorful scribbles on windows surrounding us paled in comparison to the excitement within us. We shared a strong bond: the force of changemakers.

The energy of the first class was akin to a buzzing beehive. All of us were exchanging ideas, scribbling thoughts of change we would like to implement, and getting to know each other. We were prepared for the hard work ahead of us: writing our personal stories, editing our articles and publishing the book. Our passion to make our world a better place was fueling our mission.

In the previous pages, you had the chance to read unconventional yet inspiring personal stories. During the ten intense weeks of gearing up for the production of this book, we watched movies and we typed up written work of revolutionary change. We were preparing to share a part of who we are, with you. Our vision and motivation is to empower change for the next generation.

The topics in this book span from the seriousness of educational equality to the unfettering of sexual conversations. It is everything that is important to us. It is a way to prove that our generation has the passion and ambition to make an everlasting impact. It is something that encapsulates our hopes and dreams for the world. To encase our youth by touching the lives of others is our goal.

Before taking this course, we were all regular students juggling the stresses of college. Social responsibilities, exams, grades, and sleep demanded our attention. Yet, there was a beckoning voice inside us. This desire, a quiet yearning, enticed us to make a difference. The world around us was shaped by people encouraging change, and we wanted to be a part of that creation.

Deep down, as changemakers, we knew that a struggle would arise. We expected it, the questioning reality of "Are we good enough?" The success of our vision required us to grow as communicators. To publish this book with one dynamic voice of college changemakers. As a class we paired up into groups, divided by our strengths. The writing team ate gummy bears while outlining the individual bio content.

Keyboard taps could be heard from the corner where the typesetting team was planning the font size. None of the editing team is from Chicago, yet the decided citation preference was decided by them. From time to time a subtle snap could be heard of a photo being taken by the marketing team. The cover design of this book was creatively illustrated by a team of two. This project was progressing as the promise of spring was approaching.

As the trees in Schenectady changed from bare to pink blossoms, winter bared us farewell. We sensed a feeling of empowerment rising as our stories came together. Week after week, we drove off campus with the little bus, ate dinner together in our 'office space', and engaged in dialogue. Our goal for this book is not only to create change, but to forward the unstoppable wave of amelioration. We are passionate about freeing, daring innovation.

The terms "Millennial" and "changemaker" now go hand in hand. A changemaker is not only someone like Martin Luther King Jr., Ghandi or Malala Yousafzai. There is a changemaker within each one of us. By writing our stories of change, a piece of each writer is immortalized within these pages. But these are not only stories of our class, these are stories of us, and you, the reader.

You are a changemaker when you speak out for the change you want to see in the world. Turn the inspirational feeling after reading the shared narratives into concrete action. Find what excites you, what makes the hair on your skin stand up. Do something with that feeling. Create your own story of change. Empower yourself to be part of the generation of change.

THE AUTHORS

To Christine

Most importantly, a special thanks to Professor Christine Henseler for being ambitious and driven enough to make this book happen. This absolutely could not have been done without your support and guidance.

Christine, there aren't enough words to demonstrate what you have done for all of us. You have become my role model, mentor, therapist, and friend and for that I am eternally grateful. I hope to some day be half the woman you are. You truly have made each one of the very best versions of ourselves. Thank you for taking us on this journey and believing in us every step of the way.
Much love ~ Kate

Thank you, Professor Christine Henseler for having the vision and ability to combine a class full of many different personalities in order to make this book a reality. We could not have done it without you.

~ Randi

Professor Christine Henseler, Thank U so much for sharing your heart, ideas, and passion with our class. You inspire me to be a better human while encouraging me to find my voice. I would not be where I am today without your guidance and enthusiasm. I look forward to the day when you become extremely famous so that the entire world can benefit from your vivacious and inspiring personality.

~ Hayden

To come up with an idea is one thing, but to take an idea and run with it is no easy task. I'd like to recognize Professor Christine Henseler for the tremendous amount of effort she put into not only constructing the class, but turning the thought of creating this book into a reality. By taking action, she truly possesses the characteristics and drive we wish to inspire in our readers to promote and encourage social change for generations to come.

~ Ash

Thank you so much Professor Henseler for all that you have done for us in this class. Not only have you inspired this class to accomplish great things together, but you personally inspired me to find what change I want to see in the world, which in turn has opened many doors for me to study abroad to actually take action. This all did not seem possible to do when you told us that we would be publishing a book Week 1, but seeing how far we have gone through your guidance, mentorship, and trust, is amazing and I am so grateful to you.

~ Lola

Thanks so much for providing us with such an unconventionally fun class. It took a while, but we made it all work in the end.

~ JP

Without your energy, charisma or love, none of this incredibly memorable project would have ever come to life. Thank you for all your devotion, time and consideration throughout the 10 weeks! You really were the driving force behind this project.

~ Andrés

I greatly appreciate your genuine excitement towards learning and seeing your students succeed. You made this class unfor-gettable! Your "unconventional" way of teaching is admirable, and I wish more professors would follow your lead. Thank you for believing in us and in this project.

~ Phoebe

Christine, you have given us all the energy and enthusiasm to be the most resourceful Millennial Changemakers we are capable of being. Without your spontaneity and drive, we could have never written a book, let alone a book like this one. You have given me the courage to share my story: something with which I have been restrained for years. By participating in this course, I have realized we all share a shared narrative of the human experience and have unrestrained hope for our generation and generations to come out of innate goodness. Our class has grown and identified with each other's stories, making us feel less alone and afraid to share what we harbor in our hearts. Without you, none of this would have happened. Thank you for being a professor we will never forget.

~ E.A.

Thank you so much Professor Henseler! Your energy and enthusiasm was always inspiring and I appreciate everything you did for our class. It was so different than classes I've taken in the past, and I loved the unconventional way in which it was taught. I learned a lot about myself and will remember this class for years to come. Thank you so much for everything you did to make this happen (and for all the candy too!).

~ Anna Mahony

Christine, when I registered for this course I had no idea the impact it would have on my life. I was surprised by how

I was opening up to you and your reactions were so genuine and sadly new that they brought me to tears. Thank you for your kindness and for creating this course. I have learned so much more than how to interview, write a feature article, and typeset. I have learned to open up and put trust in those around me, collaborate on a large scale, and be apart of a larger vision. I look forward to reading this book 5, 10, and 15 years from now and seeing what we have all done to pursue our passion for social change.

Thank you ~ Brooke

Thank You Christine for taking the time to develop a personal relationship with me. It truly made a difference to feel comfortable and at ease at all times around you! I was able to develop so much more because of that! From Ithaca to Schenectady I always feel at home around you!

~ Giuseppe

Christine - Many many thanks for not only being an outstanding professor, but also a one-of-a-kind friend. You believed in me and made me feel comfortable while I was vulnerable. You had a much larger impact on me than what it says in your job description, and that doesn't happen often. This class has been an experience that I hold very close to my heart, and for that I will always be grateful.

Much love ~ Megan

Christine, Thank you for being one of my favorite professors of all time here at Union College. You have given me the opportunity to really grow as a student and as a writer. Your creative and unique approach to teaching allowed me to explore my abilities and feel more confident in my writing. I'm sad to part ways with this class and you. I hope your future students go on to appreciate you as much as I did.

Thanks for everything ~ Kaitlyn Connor

Christine, I did not think that when I went into your office one day with questions about Spanish grammar that I would end up leaving having agreed to take a course with an intimidating title and ambiguous description. However, taking this class has been the highlight of my year and, to be honest, I am slightly worried that no course will ever top it. Through your guidance and open conversation, the typical college student "I don't know what I want to do with my life" dilemma seems less daunting and, instead, exciting. You have pushed us out of our comfort zones, forced us to be okay with vulnerability, and encouraged us to try to do something great, even if we might fail. And, perhaps most importantly, you have shown us that our voices are important and, by making them heard, we can effect real change. Thank you for being you.

With love ~ Kathleen

165   Generation Now: Millennials Call for Social Change

NOTES

[1] Stephanie Zacharek, "TIME Person of the Year 2017," *TIME*, 2017, http://time.com/time-person-of-the-year-2017-silence-breakers/.

[2] Holly Kearl, "The Facts Behind the #MeToo Movement: A National Study on Sexual Harassment and Assault," *Stop Street Harassment* (2018): 9. http://www.stopstreetharassment.org/wp-content/uploads/2018/01/Full-Report-2018-National-Study-on-Sexual-Harassment-and-Assault.pdf.

[3] Kearl, "The Facts Behind the #MeToo Movement: A National Study on Sexual Harassment and Assault," 14, http://www.stopstreetharassment.org/wp-content/uploads/2018/01/Full-Report-2018-National-Study-on-Sexual-Harassment-and-Assault.pdf.

[4] Kearl, "The Facts Behind the #MeToo Movement: A National Study on Sexual Harassment and Assault," 27.

[5] Shannan Catalano, "Intimate Partner Violence: Attributes of Victimization, 1993-2011," *U.S. Department of Justice* (2013): 1, https://www.bjs.gov/content/pub/pdf/ipvav9311.pdf.

[6] Natacha Godbout et al, "Early Exposure to Violence, Relationship Violence, and Relationship Satisfaction in Adolescents and Emerging Adults: The Role of Romantic Attachment," *Psychological Trauma: Theory, Research, Practice, and Policy* 9, no. 2 (2017): 134-135, DOI: 10.1037/tra0000136.

[7] Maria Puente. "Does your Generation Determine how You Perceive Sexual Harassment?" *USA Today* (2017): https://www.usatoday.com/story/life/2017/11/06/millennials-vs-genx-vs-boomers-sexual-harassment-they-different/814056001/.

[8] Rachel Schwartz and Eileen Gaffney, "Meet the (Millennial) Parents: A Whitepaper Exploring the First-Generation of Digitally Native Moms & Dads," *Crowdtap, the People-Powered Marketing Platform* (2015): http://go.crowdtap.com/DownloadReport.

9 Council on Foreign Relations. "Timeline: U.S. Postwar Immigration Policy." *Council on Foreign Relations*. Last modified 2017. https://www.cfr.org/timeline/timeline-us-postwar-immigration-policy.

10 History.com Staff. "U.S. Immigration Since 1965." History.com. Last modified 2010. https://www.history.com/topics/us-immigration-since-1965.

11 Ibid.

12 Ibid.

13 Valdez, Carmen R., Jessa Lewis Valentine, and Brian Padilla. ""Why we stay": Immigrants' Motivations for Remaining in Communities Impacted by Anti-Immigration Policy." *Cultural Diversity and Ethnic Minority Psychology* 19, no. 3 (2013): 289.

14 López, Gustavo, and Kristen Bialik. "Key Findings About U.S. Immigrants." *Pew Research Center*. Last modified May 3, 2017. http://www.pewresearch.org/fact-tank/2017/05/03/key-findings-about-u-s-immigrants/.

15 Make the Road New York. Accessed May 8, 2018. https://maketheroadny.org/.

16 Jordan Peterson, *Jordan Peterson Debate on the Gender Pay Gap*. Performed by Channel 4 News. (2018; London: YouTube, 2018), Web.

17 Sheryl Sandberg, Why We Have Too Few Women Leaders | Sheryl Sandberg. Performed by TEDTalks. (2010; YouTube, 2010), Web.

18 Ibid.

19 Ibid.

20 Jordan Peterson, *Jordan Peterson Debate on the Gender Pay Gap*. Performed by Channel 4 News. (2018; London: YouTube, 2018), Web.

21 Jessica Deahl, "Countries Around The World Beat The U.S. On Paid Parental Leave." *NPR*, October 6, 2016. https://www.npr.org/2016/10/06/495839588/countries-around-the-world-beat-the-u-s-on-paid-parental-leave.

22 Sheryl Sandberg, Why We Have Too Few Women Leaders | Sheryl Sandberg. Performed by TEDTalks. (2010; YouTube, 2010), Web.

[23] Turkewitz, Julie, Matt Stevens, Jason M. Bailey, and Jack Begg, "Emma González Leads a Student Outcry on Guns: 'This Is the Way I Have to Grieve'." *The New York Times*, February 18, 2018, accessed May 23, 2018, https://www.nytimes.com/2018/02/18/us/emma-gonzalez-florida-shooting.html.

[24] "Gender Stereotypes: Where Do They Come from and Why Do They Persist?" *Media Savvy Girls.* Accessed June 02, 2018. http://mediasavvygirls.com/gender-stereotypes-where-do-they-come-from-and-why-do-they-persist/.

[25] Covert, Bryce. "Why It Matters That Women Do Most of the Housework." *The Nation,* June 29, 2015. Accessed June 02, 2018. https://www.thenation.com/article/why-it-matters-women-do-most-housework/.

[26] Covert, Bryce. "Why It Matters That Women Do Most of the Housework." *The Nation,* June 29, 2015. Accessed June 02, 2018. https://www.thenation.com/article/why-it-matters-women-do-most-housework/.

[27] York, Catherine. "Women Dominate Journalism Schools, but Newsrooms Are Still a Different Story." *Poynter,* September 18, 2017. Accessed June 02, 2018. https://www.poynter.org/news/women-dominate-journalism-schools-newsrooms-are-still-different-story.

[28] "Gender Stereotypes: Where Do They Come from and Why Do They Persist?" *Media Savvy Girls,* Accessed June 02, 2018. http://mediasavvygirls.com/gender-stereotypes-where-do-they-come-from-and-why-do-they-persist/.

[29] Ibid.

[30] "School Age Program." *The Children's Center at UCP of Long Island,* Accessed May 6, 2018. http://www.thechildrenscenter-ucp.org/schoolage.html.

[31] "The Condition of Education - Preprimary, Elementary, and Secondary Education - Elementary and Secondary Enrollment - Children and Youth With Disabilities - Indicator April (2018)." *National Center for Education Statistics* last modified April, 2018. https://nces.ed.gov/programs/coe/indicator_cgg.asp.

[32] Ibid.

33 "School Age Program." *The Children's Center at UCP of Long Island.* Accessed May 6, 2018. http://www.thechildrenscenter-ucp.org/schoolage.html.

34 Ibid.

35 "The Condition of Education - Preprimary, Elementary, and Secondary Education - Elementary and Secondary Enrollment - Children and Youth With Disabilities - Indicator April (2018)." *National Center for Education Statistics.* Last modified April, 2018 https://nces.ed.gov/programs/coe/indicator_cgg.asp.

36 "School Age Program." *The Children's Center at UCP of Long Island.* Accessed May 6, 2018. http://www.thechildrenscenter-ucp.org/schoolage.html.

37 "School Age Program." *The Children's Center at UCP of Long Island.* Accessed May 6, 2018. http://www.thechildrenscenter-ucp.org/schoolage.html.

38 *13 Reasons Why.* Created by Brian Yorkey. 2017. Netflix, Film

39 "Suicide Statistics." *American Foundation for Suicide Prevention, Reports from 2016.* Accessed May 16, 2018, https://afsp.org/about-suicide/suicide-statistics/

40 Phineas Rueckert, "10 Barriers to Education Around the World." *Global Citizen.* https://www.globalcitizen.org/en/content/10-barriers-to-education-around-the-world-2/

41 Liesbet Steer and Katie Smith, "It's Time to Reverse Declining ODA to Education", Education Plus Development https://www.brookings.edu/blog/education-plus-development/2015/01/12/its-time-to-reverse-declining-oda-to-education/

42 Phineas Rueckert, "10 Barriers to Education Around the World", *Global Citizen,* https://www.globalcitizen.org/en/content/10-barriers-to-education-around-the-world-2/

43 Ibid.

44 *Pencils of Promise.* Accessed May 29th 2018. https://pencilsofpromise.org

45 Ibid.

46 Mercedes García-Escribano, Baoping Shang, and Emmanouil (Manos) Kitsios, "Chart of the Week: Inequality, Your Health, and Fiscal Policy", *IMF Blog*, https://blogs.imf.org/2018/02/05/chart-of-the-week-inequality-your-health-and-fiscal-policy/

47 Corinne Abrams, "How Trash Is Adding to Delhi's Air Pollution Problems," *The Wall Street Journal*, November 03, 2015, accessed May 30, 2018, https://blogs.wsj.com/indiarealtime/2015/11/03/how-trash-is-adding-to-delhis-air-pollution-problems/.

48 The World Air Quality Index Project, "Air Quality Index Scale and Color Legend," *Aqicn.org*, 2016, , accessed May 30, 2018, http://aqicn.org/scale/.

49 WHO, "Ambient Air Pollution: A Global Assessment of Exposure and Burden of Disease," World Health Organization, November 07, 2016, , accessed May 30, 2018, http://www.who.int/phe/publications/air-pollution-global-assessment/en/.

50 OECD, "The Economic Consequences of Outdoor Air Pollution," *Students, Computers and Learning - Making the Connection - En - OECD*, June 09, 2016, , accessed May 30, 2018, http://www.oecd.org/env/the-economic-consequences-of-outdoor-air-pollution-9789264257474-en.htm.

51 Ray Kurzweil, "The Law of Accelerating Returns," *Kurzweil Accelerating Intelligence*, March 07, 2001, accessed May 30, 2018, http://www.kurzweilai.net/the-law-of-accelerating-returns.

52 Ray Kurzweil, "Seeing the S-curve in Everything," *Kurzweil Accelerating Intelligence*, July 21, 2011, accessed May 30, 2018, http://www.kurzweilai.net/seeing-the-s-curve-in-everything.

53 Tyson, Neil deGrasse. "When Students Cheat on Exams It's Because our School System Values Grades More than Students Value Learning. April 14, 2013, 10:59 AM. https://twitter.com/neiltyson/status/323495818889949184?lang=en.

54 Nadia Naviwala, "What's Really Keeping Pakistan's Children Out of School?" *The New York Times*, last modified October 18, 2017, https://www.nytimes.com/2017/10/18/opinion/pakistan-education-schools.html.

55 "Pakistan is home to the most frenetic education reforms in the world," *The Economist*, last modified January 4, 2018, https://www.economist.com/briefing/2018/01/04/pakistan-is-home-to-the-most-frenetic-education-reforms-in-the-world.

56 Ibid,

57 "'Dawson's Creek' Cast Reunites for Its 20th Anniversary on This Week's EW Cover." *EW.com*. Accessed May 10, 2018. http://ew.com/tv/2018/03/28/dawsons-creek-reunion-cw-cover/.

58 Dawson's Creek. "Decisions." 13.David Semel. Mike White & Dana Baratta (teleplay), Jon Harmon Feldman (story). The WB, May 19, 1998.

59 Plaugic, Lizzie. "A Record-breaking Number of LGBTQ Characters Appeared on TV in 2017." *The Verge*. November 09, 2017. Accessed May 17, 2018. https://www.theverge.com/2017/11/9/16628754/glaad-study-tv-lgbtq-characters-diversity.

60 Bourdillon, Roxy. "Shay Mitchell: Playing a Lesbian Character Was the Best Part out of Everything." *Diva Magazine*. Accessed May 30, 2018. http://www.divamag.co.uk/Diva-Magazine/Celebs/Shay-Mitchell-Playing-a-lesbian-character-was-the-best-part-out-of-everything/.

61 Tate, Allison Slater. "Why One Man Hopes to Send Thousands of Kids to See 'Black Panther'." *TODAY.com*. January 12, 2018. Accessed May 27, 2018. https://www.today.com/parents/man-wants-send-kids-black-panther-great-reason-t121104.

62 Connolly, N.D.B. "How 'Black Panther' Taps Into 500 Years of History." *The Hollywood Reporter*. February 16, 2018. Accessed May 27, 2018. https://www.hollywoodreporter.com/heat-vision/black-panther-taps-500-years-history-1085334

63 Campbell, Christopher. "Every Record Broken by 'Black Panther'." *Fandango*. March 21, 2018. Accessed May 30, 2018. https://www.fandango.com/movie-news/every-record-broken-by-black-panther-753009.

64 "Mental Health and Schools," *Joint Action Mental Health and Wellbeing*, 2015, https://www.mentalhealthandwellbeing.eu/

[65] Marc Suhrcke, Demetris Pillas, & Caroline Selai, "Economic aspects of mental health in children and adolescents," *WHO European Office for Investment for Health and Development*, Venice, Italy, WHO Regional Office for Europe, 43-64.

[66] "Mental Health and Schools," Joint Action Mental Health and Wellbeing, 2015, https://www.mentalhealthandwellbeing.eu/.

[67] Myron L. Belfer, "Child and Adolescent Mental Disorders: the Magnitude of the Problem Across the Globe," *The Journal of Child Psychology and Psychiatry* 49, no. 3(2008): 226.

[68] *Happy Feet*, directed by George Miller (2006; Burbank, Warner Bros. Pictures), Film.

[69] Livia Albeck-Ripka, "Your Recycling Gets Recycled Right? Maybe, or Maybe Not", *The New York Times*, May 29, 2018.

[70] Paul Chapman, "Environmental Education and Sustainability in U.S. Public Schools," last accessed May 23, 2018. http://projectgreenschools.org/wp/wp-content/uploads/2014/08/USGreenSchools12114.pdf.

[71] Paul Chapman, "Environmental Education and Sustainability in U.S. Public Schools," last accessed May 23, 2018. http://projectgreenschools.org/wp/wp-content/uploads/2014/08/USGreenSchools12114.pdf.

[72] Michael Kaplowitz and Ralph Levine, "How Environmental Knowledge Measures up at a Big Ten University," *Environmental Education Research* 11, no. 2 (2005): 156, DOI: 10.1080/1350462042000338324.

[73] Michael Kaplowitz and Ralph Levine, "How environmental knowledge measures up at a Big Ten university," *Environmental Education Research* 11, no. 2 (2005): 156, DOI: 10.1080/1350462042000338324.

[74] "State Environmental Literacy Plans," *North American Association for Environmental Education*, (Washington, D.C., 2014), https://cdn.naaee.org/sites/default/files/2014-selp.2.25.15.pdf.

[75] Ibid

76 Michael Greshko et al. "A Running List of How Trump Is Changing the Environment," *National Geographic*, May 11, 2018. https://news.nationalgeographic.com/2017/03/how-trump-is-changing-science-environment/

77 Dina Spector, "New Zealand Commits to 90% Renewable Energy by 2025," *Business Insider*, September 8, 2011, http://www.businessinsider.com/new-zealand-renewable-energy-2011-09.

78 Dina Spector, "New Zealand Commits to 90% Renewable Energy by 2025," *Business Insider*, September 8, 2011, http://www.businessinsider.com/new-zealand-renewable-energy-2011-09.

79 Christopher F. Schuetze, "Dutch Supermarket Introduces Plastic-Free Aisle," *The New York Times*, February 28, 2018, https://www.nytimes.com/2018/02/28/business/netherlands-plastic-supermarket.html.

80 Melati and Isabel Wisjen, "Bye Bye Plastic Bags," *Bye Bye Plastic Bags*, last accessed May 22, 2018, http://www.byebyeplasticbags.org/about/.

81 Ibid

82 Ibid

83 "The Be Straw Free Campaign", *nps.gov*, 2013, https://www.nps.gov/commercialservices/greenline_straw_free.htm.

84 "Plastic Bag Consumption Facts", *ConservingNow*, accessed May 22, 2018, https://conservingnow.com/plastic-bag-consumption-facts/.

85 Ibid

86 Ibid

87 Saskia De Melker, "The Case for Starting Sex Education in Kindergarten," *PBS News Hour*, last modified May 27, 2015, https://www.pbs.org/newshour/health/spring-fever.

88 Matt Egan, "Record inequality: The top 1% controls 38.6% of America's wealth," *CNN*, September 27, 2017, http://money.cnn.com/2017/09/27/news/economy/inequality-record-top-1-percent-wealth/index.html.

89 Peter Osborn, "Do College Grads Really Earn More Than High School Grands?" *Cornerstone University*, November 29, 2016,https://www.cornerstone.edu/blogs/lifelong-learning-matters/post/do-college-grads-really-earn-more-than-high-school-grads.

90 Lyndsey Layton, "Majority of U.S. public school students are in poverty," *The Washington Post*, January 16, 2015, https://www.washingtonpost.com/local/education/majority-of-us-public-school-students-are-in-poverty/2015/01/15/df7171d0-9ce9-11e4-a7ee-526210d665b4_story.html?noredirect=on&utm_term=.fde404c7464f.

91 Lam T. Vo, "How Much Does The Government Spend To Send A Kid To Public School?" *NPR*, June 21, 2012, https://www.npr.org/sections/money/2012/06/21/155515613/how-much-does-the-government-spend-to-send-a-kid-to-school.

92 Layton, "Majority of U.S. Public School Students Are in Poverty," *The Washington Post*, https://www.washingtonpost.com/local/education/majority-of-us-public-school-students-are-in-poverty/2015/01/15/df7171d0-9ce9-11e4-a7ee-526210d665b4_story.html?noredirect=on&utm_term=.fde404c7464f.

93 "Criminal Justice Fact Sheet," *NAACP*, last modified 2018, http://www.naacp.org/criminal-justice-fact-sheet/.

94 "School To Prison Pipililne," *ACLU*, last modified 2018, https://www.aclu.org/issues/juvenile-justice/school-prison-pipeline.

95 "Recruiting Students: Tomorrow's Leaders Have Arrived," *The Posse Foundation*, last modified 2018, https://www.possefoundation.org/recruiting-students.

96 Skye Cowie, "How Chronic Lyme Disease Changed My Life," Global Lyme Alliance, December 1, 2017, https://globallymealliance.org/chronic-lyme-disease-changed-life/.

97 Christina Kovacs, "The Answer- My Diagnosis," *Lady of Lyme* (blog), October 27, 2011, http://www.ladyoflyme.com/blog/archives/10-2011.

98 Amy Tan, "My Plight With Lyme Disease," *The New York Times*, August 11, 2013, https://www.nytimes.com/roomfordebate/2013/08/11/deconstructing-lyme-disease/my-plight-with-lyme-disease.

99 "Protecting Students With Disabilities," *U.S. Department of Education*, accessed May 15, 2018, https://www2.ed.gov/about/offices/list/ocr/504faq.html.

BIBLIOGRAPHY

"13 Reasons Why." Netflix. March 31, 2017.

Abrams, Corinne. "How Trash Is Adding to Delhi's Air Pollution Problems." *The Wall Street Journal.* November 03, 2015. Accessed May 30, 2018. https://blogs.wsj.com/indiarealtime/2015/11/03/how-trash-is-adding-to-delhis-air-pollution-problems/.

Albeck-Ripka, L. "Your Recycling Gets Recycled Right? Maybe, or Maybe Not", *The New York Times.* May 29, 2018.

Belfer, Myron L. "Child and Adolescent Mental Disorders: The Magnitude of the Problem Across the Globe." *The Journal of Child Psychology and Psychiatry* 49, no. 3(2008): 226-236.

Bourdillon, Roxy. "Shay Mitchell: Playing a Lesbian Character Was the Best Part out of Everything." *Diva Magazine.* Accessed May 30, 2018. http://www.divamag.co.uk/Diva-Magazine/Celebs/Shay-Mitchell-Playing-a-lesbian-character-was-the-best-part-out-of-everything/.

Braun, Adam, *Pencils of Promise*, Simon and Schuster, 2014.

Campbell, Christopher. "Every Record Broken by 'Black Panther'." *Fandango.* March 21, 2018. Accessed May 30, 2018. https://www.fandango.com/movie-news/every-record-broken-by-black-panther-753009.

Catalano, Shannan. "Intimate Partner Violence: Attributes of Victimization, 1993-2011." *U.S. Department of Justice* (2013): 1-18. https://www.bjs.gov/content/pub/pdf/ipvav9311.pdf.

Channel 4 News. "Jordan Peterson Debate on the Gender Pay Gap, Campus Protests and Postmodernism." YouTube video, 29:55. January 16, 2018. https://www.youtube.com/watch?v=aMcjxSThD54.

Chapman, P. "Environmental Education and Sustainability in U.S. Public Schools." Last accessed May 23, 2018. http://projectgreenschools.org/wp/wp-content/uploads/2014/08/USGreenSchools12114.pdf.

"Climate Change 2014 Synthesis Report Fifth Assessment Report." *Intergovernmental Panel on Climate Change*. Last modified 2018. http://ar5-syr.ipcc.ch/topic_adaptation.php.

Connolly, N.D.B. "How 'Black Panther' Taps Into 500 Years of History." *The Hollywood Reporter*. February 16, 2018. Accessed May 27, 2018. https://www.hollywoodreporter.com/heat-vision/black-panther-taps-500-years-history-1085334.

Council on Foreign Relations. "Timeline: U.S. Postwar Immigration Policy." *Council on Foreign Relations*. Last modified 2017. https://www.cfr.org/timeline/timeline-us-postwar-immigration-policy.

Covert, Bryce. "Why It Matters That Women Do Most of the Housework." *The Nation*. June 29, 2015. Accessed June 02, 2018. https://www.thenation.com/article/why-it-matters-women-do-most-housework/.

Cowie, Skye. "How Chronic Lyme Disease Changed My Life." *Global Lyme Alliance*. December 1, 2017. https://globallymealliance.org/chronic-lyme-disease-changed-life/.

"Criminal Justice Fact Sheet." *NAACP*. Last modified 2018. http://www.naacp.org/criminal-justice-fact-sheet/.

"'Dawson's Creek' Cast Reunites for Its 20th Anniversary on This Week's EW Cover." *EW.com*. Accessed May 10, 2018. http://ew.com/tv/2018/03/28/dawsons-creek-reunion-ew-cover/.

Dawson's Creek. "Decisions." 13.David Semel. Mike White & Dana Baratta (teleplay) Jon Harmon Feldman (story). The WB, May 19, 1998.

Deahl, Jessica. "Countries Around The World Beat The U.S. On Paid Parental Leave." *NPR*. Last modified October 6, 2016. https://www.npr.org/2016/10/06/495839588/countries-around-the-world-beat-the-u-s-on-paid-parental-leave.

De Melker, Saskia. "The Case for Starting Sex Education in Kindergarten." *PBS News Hour*. May 27, 2015. https://www.pbs.org/newshour/health/spring-fever.

Egan, Matt. "Record inequality: The top 1% controls 38.6% of America's wealth." *CNN*. September 27, 2017. http://

money.cnn.com/2017/09/27/news/economy/inequality-record-top-1-percent-wealth/index.html.

García-Escribano, Mercedes, Shang, Baoping and Kitsios, Emmanouil, "Chart of the Week: Inequality, Your Health, and Fiscal Policy", *IMF Blog*, February 5, 2018. https://blogs.imf.org/2018/02/05/chart-of-the-week-inequality-your-health-and-fiscal-policy/.

"Gender Stereotypes: Where Do They Come from and Why Do They Persist?" *Media Savvy Girls*. Accessed June 02, 2018. http://mediasavvygirls.com/gender-stereotypes-where-do-they-come-from-and-why-do-they-persist/.

Godbout, Natacha, Marie-Ève Daspe, Yvan Lussier, Stéphane Sabourin, Don Dutton, and Martine Hébert. "Early Exposure to Violence, Relationship Violence, and Relationship Satisfaction in Adolescents and Emerging Adults: The Role of Romantic Attachment." (2017). *Psychological Trauma: Theory, Research, Practice, and Policy*, 9 (2), 127-137. http://dx.doi.org/10.1037/tra0000136

Greshko, Michael, Laura Parker, and Brian Clark Howard. "A Running List of How Trump Is Changing the Environment." *National Geographic* (May 11, 2018). https://news.nationalgeographic.com/2017/03/how-trump-is-changing-science-environment.

Haskins, Ron. "Three Simple Rules Poor Teens Should Follow to Join the Middle Class." *Brookings Institute*. July 28, 2016. Accessed May 25, 2018. https://www.brookings.edu/opinions/three-simple-rules-poor-teens-should-follow-to-join-the-middle-class/.

History.com Staff. "U.S. Immigration Since 1965." *History.com*. Last modified 2010. https://www.history.com/topics/us-immigration-since-1965.

Kaplowitz, Michael, and Ralph Levine. "How Environmental Knowledge Measures up at a Big Ten University." *Environmental Education Research* 11, no. 2 (2005): 143-160. Professional Development Collection. EBSCOhost (accessed May 22, 2018).DOI: 10.1080 /135046 20420003 38324.

Kearl, Holly. "The Facts Behind the #MeToo Movement: A National Study on Sexual Harassment and Assault." *Stop Street Harassment* (2018): 1-38. http://

www.stopstreetharassment.org/wp-content/uploads/2018/01/Full-Report-2018-National-Study-on-Sexual-Harassment-and-Assault.pdf.

Kurzweil, Ray. "Seeing the S-curve in Everything." *Kurzweil Accelerating Intelligence.* July 21, 2011. Accessed May 30, 2018. http://www.kurzweilai.net/seeing-the-s-curve-in-everything.

Kurzweil, Ray. "The Law of Accelerating Returns." *Kurzweil Accelerating Intelligence.* March 07, 2001. Accessed May 30, 2018. http://www.kurzweilai.net/the-law-of-accelerating-returns.

Layton, Lyndsey. "Majority of U.S. public school students are in poverty." *The Washington Post.* January 16, 2015. https://www.washingtonpost.com/local/education/majority-of-us-public-school-students-are-in-poverty/2015/01/15/df7171d0-9ce9-11e4-a7ee-526210d665b4_story.html?noredirect=on&utm_term=.fde404c7464f.

López, Gustavo, and Kristen Bialik. "Key Findings About U.S. Immigrants." *Pew Research Center.* Last modified May 3, 2017. http://www.pewresearch.org/fact-tank/2017/05/03/key-findings-about-u-s-immigrants/.

Make the Road New York. Accessed May 8, 2018. https://maketheroadny.org/.

"Mental Health and Schools." *Joint Action Mental Health and Wellbeing.* 2015. https://www.mentalhealthandwellbeing.eu/

Miller, George, dir. Happy Feet. 2006; Burbank: Warner Bros. Pictures. Film. "Plastic Bag Consumption Facts." *ConservingNow.* Accessed May 22, 2018. https://conservingnow.com/plastic-bag-consumption-facts/.

Naviwala, Nadia. "What's Really Keeping Pakistan's Children Out of School?" *The New York Times.* Last modified October 18, 2017. https://www.nytimes.com/2017/10/18/opinion/pakistan-education-schools.html.

OECD. "The Economic Consequences of Outdoor Air Pollution." *Students, Computers and Learning - Making the Connection - En - OECD.* June 09, 2016. Accessed May 30, 2018. http://www.oecd.org/env/the-economic-consequences-of-outdoor-air-pollution-9789264257474-en.htm.

Osborn, Peter. "Do College Grads Really Earn More Than High School Grands?" *Cornerstone University*. November 29, 2016. https://www.cornerstone.edu/blogs/lifelong-learning-matters/post/do-college-grads-really-earn-more-than-high-school-grads.

"Pakistan is home to the most frenetic education reforms in the world." The Economist. Last modified January 4, 2018. https://www.economist.com/briefing/2018/01/04/pakistan-is-home-to-the-most-frenetic-education-reforms-in-the-world.

Plaugic, Lizzie. "A Record-breaking Number of LGBTQ Characters Appeared on TV in 2017." The Verge. November 09, 2017. Accessed May 17, 2018. https://www.theverge.com/2017/11/9/16628754/glaad-study-tv-lgbtq-characters-diversity.

"Protecting Students With Disabilities." U.S. Department of Education. Accessed May 15, 2018. https://www2.ed.gov/about/offices/list/ocr/504faq.html#introduction.

Psychological Trauma: Theory, Research, Practice, and Policy 9, no. 2 (2017): 127-137. DOI: 10.1037/ta0000136.

Puente, Maria. "Does your generation determine how you perceive sexual harassment?" USA Today (2017): https://www.usatoday.com/story/life/2017/11/06/millennials-vs-genx-vs-boomers-sexual-harassment-they-different/814056001/.

"Recruiting Students: Tomorrow's Leaders Have Arrived." The Posse Foundation. Last modified 2018. https://www.possefoundation.org/recruiting-students.

Rueckert, Phineas, "10 Barriers to Education Around the World", Global Citizen, January 24, 2018. https://www.globalcitizen.org/en/content/10-barriers-to-education-around-the-world-2/.

"School Age Program." The Children's Center at UCP of Long Island. Accessed May 6, 2018. http://www.thechildrenscenter-ucp.org/schoolage.html.

"School To Prison Pipeline." ACLU. Last modified 2018. https://www.aclu.org/issues/juvenile-justice/school-prison-pipeline.

Schuetze, C. F. "Dutch Supermarket Introduces Plastic-Free Aisle." The New York Times. February 28, 2018. https://www.nytimes.com/2018/02/28/business/netherlands-plastic-supermarket.html.

Schwartz, Rachel and Eileen Gaffney. "Meet the (Millennial) Parents: A Whitepaper Exploring the First-Generation of Digitally Native Moms & Dads." Crowdtap, the People-Powered Marketing Platform (2015): http://go.crowdtap.com/DownloadReport.

Smith, Katie and Steer, Liesbet, "It's Time to Reverse Declining ODA to Education", Education Plus Development, January 12, 2015. https://www.brookings.edu/blog/education-plus-development/2015/01/12/its-time-to-reverse-declining-oda-to-education/.

Spector, D. "New Zealand Commits to 90% Renewable Energy by 2025." Business Insider. September 8, 2011. http://www.businessinsider.com/new-zealand-renewable-energy-2011-09.

"State Environmental Literacy Plans." North American Association for Environmental Education. (Washington, D.C., 2014). https://cdn.naaee.org/sites/default/files/2014-selp.2.25.15.pdf.

Steward, Melissa. "The Father Absence Crisis in America [Infographic]." Father Involvement Programs for Organizations and Families. Accessed May 25, 2018. https://www.fatherhood.org/the-father-absence-crisis-in-america.

Suhrcke, M., Pillas, D., & Selai, C. "Economic aspects of mental health in children and adolescents." WHO European Office for Investment for Health and Development, Venice, Italy, WHO Regional Office for Europe. 43-64.

"Suicide Statistics." American Foundation for Suicide Prevention. Reports from 2016. Accessed May 16, 2018. https://afsp.org/about-suicide/suicide-statistics/.

Tan, Amy. "My Plight With Lyme Disease." The New York Times. August 11, 2013. https://www.nytimes.com/roomfordebate/2013/08/11/deconstructing-lyme-disease/my-plight-with-lyme-disease.

Tate, Allison Slater. "Why One Man Hopes to Send Thousands of Kids to See 'Black Panther'." TODAY.com. January 12, 2018.

Accessed May 27, 2018. https://www.today.com/parents/man-wants-send-kids-black-panther-great-reason-t121104.

TEDTalks. "Why We Have Too Few Women Leaders | Sheryl Sandberg." YouTube video, 15:28. December 21, 2010. https://www.youtube.com/watch?v=18uDutylDa4.

"The Be Straw Free Campaign." nps.gov. 2013. https://www.nps.gov/commercialservices/greenline_straw_free.htm.

"The Condition of Education - Preprimary, Elementary, and Secondary Education - Elementary and Secondary Enrollment - Children and Youth With Disabilities - Indicator April (2018)." National Center for Education Statistics. Last modified April, 2018. https://nces.ed.gov/programs/coe/indicator_cgg.asp.

Turkewitz, Julie, Matt Stevens, Jason M. Bailey, and Jack Begg. "Emma González Leads a Student Outcry on Guns: 'This Is the Way I Have to Grieve'." The New York Times. February 18, 2018. Accessed May 23, 2018. https://www.nytimes.com/2018/02/18/us/emma-gonzalez-florida-shooting.html.

Tyson, Neil deGrasse. "When Students Cheat on Exams it's Because our School System Values Grades more than Students Value Learning." April 14, 2013, 10:59 AM. https://twitter.com/neiltyson/status/323495818889949184?lang=en.

Valdez, Carmen R., Jessa Lewis Valentine, and Brian Padilla. ""Why we stay": Immigrants' Motivations for Remaining in Communities Impacted by Anti-Immigration Policy." *Cultural Diversity and Ethnic Minority Psychology* 19, no. 3 (2013): 289.

Vo, Lam T. "How Much Does The Government Spend To Send A Kid To Public School?" NPR. June 21, 2012. https://www.npr.org/sections/money/2012/06/21/155515613/how-much-does-the-government-spend-to-send-a-kid-to-school.

Wisjen, Melati and Isabel Wisjen. "Bye Bye Plastic Bags." *Bye Bye Plastic Bags*. Last accessed May 22, 2018. http://www.byebyeplasticbags.org/about/.

WHO. "Ambient Air Pollution: A Global Assessment of Exposure and Burden of Disease." *World Health Organization*.

November 07, 2016. Accessed May 30, 2018. http://www.who.int/phe/publications/air-pollution-global-assessment/en/.

World Air Quality Index Project. "Air Quality Index Scale and Color Legend." *Aqicn.org*. 2016. Accessed May 30, 2018. http://aqicn.org/scale/.

York, Catherine. "Women Dominate Journalism Schools, but Newsrooms Are Still a Different Story." *Poynter*. September 18, 2017. Accessed June 02, 2018. https://www.poynter.org/news/women-dominate-journalism-schools-newsrooms-are-still-different-story.

Zacharek, Stephanie, Eliana Dockterman, and Haley Sweetland Edwards. "TIME Person of the Year 2017: The Silence Breakers." *TIME* (2017): http://time.com/time-person-of-the-year-2017-silence-breakers/.

185   Generation Now: Millennials Call for Social Change

186   Generation Now: Millennials Call for Social Change